Throughout her menstrual cycle, during the reproductive years, a woman's body displays various signs and symptoms of fertility which can be observed and interpreted. Once recognised, this fertility awareness can be used with increasing accuracy to estimate ovulation, leaving the woman with the choice of avoiding or planning a pregnancy.

A Manual of Natural Family Planning describes each of the main indicators of fertility – basal body temperature changes, the presence/absence plus amount/consistency of cervical mucus, changes in the cervix itself – and also those minor physical changes common to many women. When she has learnt to observe and record those signs particularly indicative of her cycle, using the double-check method, a woman can be confident of the knowledge she now has about her own fertility because the method selected is tailor-made to suit her requirements.

The benefits of fertility awareness are far-reaching: to avoid conception, to plan and achieve a pregnancy, to understand the internal activity which may give rise to pre-menstrual tension, to realise what's happening during puberty or at menopause. A knowledge of how our bodies work can help us feel more in control and able to cope with physical and emotional changes throughout each cycle.

This book, requested by many women and men who have already decided to find out about the way in which fertility awareness can be exploited to their advantage, will also serve as an excellent introduction to anyone who is interested or intrigued by Natural Family Planning methods, whilst teachers and users of the method will find it invaluable for reference.

Dr Anna Flynn is an Obstetrician and Gynaecologist with special research and training in fertility awareness. She was the principal investigator for the World Health Organisation's pilot study in Natural Family Planning teaching and has been the consultant for training programmes throughout the world. In 1982 she co-founded the National Association for Natural Family Planning Teachers in England and Wales. Currently based at the Queen Elizabeth Hospital, Birmingham, sh̶e ̶ ̶ ̶ ̶es to research, and conducts N̶ ̶ ̶ ̶ ̶ ̶ ̶ ̶ g programmes in the UK an̶ ̶

Melissa Brooks is a Sociol̶ ̶ ̶ ̶ ̶ ̶ ̶ ̶ ̶ ̶ f Durham. She worked fo̶ ̶ ̶ ̶ ̶ ̶ ̶ ̶ ̶ ̶ concentrating her interest̶ ̶ ̶ ̶ ̶ ̶ ̶ ̶ editor and writer.

A MANUAL OF
NATURAL FAMILY
PLANNING

Dr Anna M Flynn &
Melissa Brooks

UNWIN
PAPERBACKS

LONDON SYDNEY WELLINGTON

First published in Great Britain by George Allen & Unwin 1984

First published in paperback by Unwin®Paperbacks, an imprint of
Unwin Hyman Limited in 1985
Reprinted 1988
New edition 1990

UNWIN HYMAN LIMITED
15/17 Broadwick Street, London W1V 1FP

George Allen & Unwin Australia Pty Ltd
8 Napier Street, North Sydney, NSW 2060, Australia

Unwin Paperbacks New Zealand Pty Ltd with Port Nicholson Press
Compusales Building, 75 Ghuznee Street, Wellington, New Zealand

A CIP catalogue record for this book is available from the British Library.

ISBN 0 04 176008 5

Printed in Great Britain by Guernsey Press Co,
Guernsey, Channel Islands

Contents

Acknowledgements

Acknowledgements are due to the World Health Organisation and the British Life Assurance Trust for use of material from the Family Fertility Education Learning Package; to Unipath, Bedford; Bioself Distributors Ltd, Geneva; Monoclonal Antibodies Inc., California; Cerviscope of Cerviscreen, Guildford for the cervix photographs and to Dr J. A. Menezes for use of the cervical mucus photographs, taken from *Natural Family Planning in Pictures* (Catholic Hospital Association of India, 1980).

With thanks also to Laura McKechnie for the line illustrations.

Preface: Dr Anna Flynn

As an Obstetrician and Gynaecologist, I have had close contact with women and couples in the delicate and reserved area of sexuality and fertility. I have worked in developing countries as well as in our sophisticated Western society with people of all ages and social classes, at both ends of the reproductive spectrum – helping some to bring their babies into the world, others to space or limit their families and others less fertile and less fortunate eventually to know the joys of pregnancy and parenthood. This first experience showed me that our heterogeneous society, from the illiterate Hottentot in the Kalahari desert to the highly educated professional in the West, was united by awe and ignorance about the cycle of fertility and reproduction. The joy and gratitude expressed by those whom I had the opportunity to teach about fertility and natural family planning was for me highly rewarding, and my efforts were further stimulated by their oft-repeated phrase 'I wish I had known that when I was younger'.

Later, as a research worker in Reproductive Physiology, I discovered that women, when taught to make simple personal observations, could almost intuitively predict when they were fertile as successfully as could the research workers in the laboratory.

Finally, I found that psychological and emotional traits in women are intimately related to their fertility. Very often they do not understand the peaks and troughs consequent on the powerful ebb and flow of the reproductive hormones during the cycle, and nor do their sexual partners. A knowledge of fertility and how it works brings not only enlightenment but a sense of relief at understanding oneself and being understood.

All these experiences prompted me to put the fundamental facts into a book in order to reach all those still seeking an explanation for their bodily vibes. *A Manual of*

Natural Family Planning is therefore a book for women. It is not a scientific treatise but a sharing of this awareness of our bodies which is common to all women. May they have as much pleasure in reading it as I have had in writing it.

This book is also written for men. It is only through a knowledge of each other's different but complementary fertilities, psychologies and emotions that communication and response are developed in the partnership. This is, I believe, a good foundation for a happy family.

I hope, therefore, that in reading this book couples of any cultural, racial or religious background will find the necessary information to make informed choices for themselves, in their relationships with others and in their families.

1

What is natural family planning?

The problem of how to control fertility has taxed people's imaginations for centuries. In this age of technological advance, modern science has discovered several artificial methods of regulating conception, from the sheath and the diaphragm to the intrauterine device (IUD) and the oral contraceptive pill, all of which have varying degrees of success.

Despite this, more and more women today are expressing a real disenchantment with the available artificial methods of contraception. Some are turning instead to the possibilities offered by the so-called 'natural' methods of family planning, and it is interesting to speculate on their reasons for doing so.

The last decade has witnessed a universal upsurge of disillusionment with the 'age of plastics' and a growing realisation, especially among young people, of the wisdom of learning to live in harmony with nature rather than at war with it. The rapid growth of the ecological movement, both in the UK ad abroad, bears testimony to this. So, too, does the current emphasis on 'healthy' living, the need for a good diet and plenty of exercise, the positive benefits of natural methods of childbirth and breast feeding, together with a growing reluctance to turn to the pill bottle to ease every ache and pain. All are expressions of the growing desire of women and men to regain control of their own lives and set their bodies free from the tyranny of technology.

Also, with the passage of time more becomes known about the adverse side-effects of some of the artificial methods of contraception. The potential health risks associated with the contraceptive pill have been much discussed, both in the medical journals and the popular press, over the last few years, and fresh evidence of the dangers to health posed by the pill, especially for long-term users and women in their thirties or older, appears regularly. Many women obviously feel that these dangers now outweigh the convenience of the pill: in 1978 a study conducted by the Family Planning Association showed that in England and Wales 0.5 million women – one-seventh of the total users – had stopped taking the pill that year.

More recently, a chart produced by the United Nations Secretariat on world contraceptive use in 1987 shows that, on average, 25% of couples in the reproductive age group in developed countries rely on 'non-supply' methods, i.e. rhythm and/or withdrawal, for contraception. In more detail the statistics for the United Kingdom show that although only 7% of women use the IUD, 'non-supply' methods are used by 8%.

The desire of many modern women to liberate their bodies from the dictates of drugs and doctors has led some to take a close look at the natural methods of family planning. In the past, ignorance and distrust made members of the medical profession, and consequently their clients, reject natural methods, but this situation is now changing, largely as a result of public demand and modern scientific discoveries about how the reproductive system works.

Today, natural methods are being increasingly and successfully used by couples in western cultures, not as in preceding decades for moral or religious reasons, but for reasons of ecology and health.

Nature has provided women with a highly effective, built-in system of fertility regulation. The goal for users of natural family planning is to utilise this natural birth control system and so eliminate the need for artificial inputs to the body. Surprisingly few women realise that they are able to conceive for only a few days each month and that it is possible, with increasing accuracy, to gauge the timing and duration of that fertile time.

In simple terms, natural family planning means becoming aware of the body's reproductive processes, both in women and men, and then learning to observe and record the natural signs and symptoms of fertility that every woman experiences during her menstrual cycles. As these signs can correctly identify the woman's fertile time, the couple are then free to decide together either to abstain from sexual intercourse if they wish to avoid a pregnancy or, if they wish to have a child, they can be assured that this is the optimum time for achieving conception. In this way, natural family planning offers a risk-free, reliable and, most important of all, a positive approach to family planning.

Science has played its part in the changing attitudes to natural family planning. In the past it was argued that natural family planning methods lacked a sound scientific foundation and that they depended on an unreliable combination of guesswork, old wives' tales and almost permanent abstinence from sexual pleasures. An understandably offputting image! In the light of the extensive scientific research carried out in many countries over the last decade, such criticisms are no longer valid. There is now a greatly improved understanding of the intricacies of the processes of human reproduction and fertility, and this has led to the development of much more precise and therefore reliable methods of family planning – methods that are devised to work with, rather than against, the natural cycles of a woman's body.

The history of natural family planning

Traditionally, in all societies and cultures a woman's fertility has been associated with the menstrual cycle. In the Old Testament, the Book of Leviticus and others make frequent reference to a woman's fertile period, laying

3

down strict rules for the legal purity of women. According to these prescriptions, menstruation was not considered a fertile time; rather, the fertile time was believed to occur about the middle of the cycle. The theories of female fertility in the following centuries show just how advanced this early thinking was.

The earliest mention of periodic abstinence to prevent pregnancy is attributed to the Greek physician Soranus of Ephesus, who practised medicine in Rome in AD 98–138. His knowledge of reproductive physiology led him to believe, somewhat erroneously, that conception was most likely to occur immediately after menstruation, when the womb had been 'scraped clean' ready for the male seed to attach itself to the wall of the womb. He therefore recommended that if pregnancy was to be avoided, the couple should abstain from sexual intercourse during the last days of menstruation and the days immediately following – advice which, if followed, greatly increases the likelihood of conception!

This physiological misconception of equating menstruation with fertility persisted through the nineteenth century (see Table 1), and, in fact, was not corrected until the 1930s. Independent studies by Ogino (1930) in Japan and Knaus (1933) in Austria demonstrated that conception can only occur during a brief period between menstrual cycles around the time of ovulation. They also showed that, regardless of the length of the menstrual cycle, the time between ovulation and the next menstruation is usually fairly consistent. Using this discovery, both Ogino and Knaus developed formulae to determine the fertile and infertile days in a woman's cycle. This formed the basis of the calendar or rhythm method of family planning, whereby planned sexual intercourse or abstinence during the fertile time a pregnancy could be achieved or avoided. During the decades following the discovery, this method, although not very effective, enjoyed widespread popularity.

In the late 1930s and 1940s rapid advances were made in detecting the effects of the sex hormones present in the woman's body at different times in the menstrual cycle.

What is natural family planning?

The insights gained from these discoveries led to further developments in natural family planning methods.

In 1939 two French doctors, Palmer and Devillers, found that a sudden increase or shift in the woman's body temperature occurred during the menstrual cycle. Further investigation led them to the conclusion that this temperature shift coincided with the time of ovulation and so could be used to indicate when the fertile time for that cycle was over. This theory formed the basis of the temperature or thermal method of natural planning, first described by Férin, a Belgian gynaecologist, in 1947 and found to be more efficient than the calendar method. In the following years various combinations of temperature and calendar calculations were proposed. These are known as the calculothermal methods of natural family planning.

Table 1

Year	Researcher	Theory
1672	Kerkring	Women eject ova above all during menstruation, or on being vehemently angry
1821	Power	Menstruation is connected with the generative faculty
1831	Lee	All the phenomena of menstruation depend upon, or are connected with some change in the ovaries
1839	Gendrin	Every functional bleeding is correlated with the expulsion of the mature ovum
1840	Negrier	Relationship of cause to effect exists between the ovarian follicle and menstruation
1843	Girdwood	The capability for impregnation is, during menstruation, at its apex
1845	Pouchet	Menstruation in women is equal to being on heat in animals
1852	Letheby	Ovules escape from the ovaries of women during the menstrual discharge
1854	Bischoof	Women ovulate at the time of menstruation
1866	Trall	Menstruation is ovulation

(Adapted from the *History of the Biologic Control of Human Fertility* by Jan Mucharski.)

Another natural sign of fertility to be investigated was the mucus produced by the neck of the womb (the cervix).

Experiments conducted by Seguy and Vimeux in 1933 revealed a direct relationship between changes in the quality and quantity of cervical mucus and the fertile and infertile phases of the menstrual cycle. Later studies confirmed this link, showing that the peak secretions of mucus coincided with the time of high fertility.

It was not until 1964 that these discoveries were applied to methods of natural family planning, when a husband and wife team from Australia, Drs John and Evelyn Billings, developed a set of rules for observing cervical mucus as a means of identifying the fertile phase of the cycle. They maintained that women could be taught to observe and record the changes in their mucus pattern through the course of the menstrual cycle and to use this to identify the beginning and end of the fertile phase. This is known as the ovulation or Billings method of natural family planning.

Research is still continuing to improve natural methods of family planning, particularly in an attempt to obtain a more precise definition of the length of the fertile phase and also to discover more about the lifespan of the sperm once they have entered the woman's reproductive system. Efforts are also being made on the technological front to find simple 'do-it-yourself' kits to make identification of the fertile days as foolproof and accurate as possible. Scientists are working on a number of devices which are sensitive to the physical changes in the woman's body, though research still has some way to go. Some of this research is discussed in Chapter 9.

Fertility awareness

Natural family planning has two separate components. The recognition of the fertile and infertile phases of the menstrual cycle is the first requisite and essential for the practice of natural methods. This involves observing the natural signs and symptoms that a woman's body displays as indicators of the phases of the cycle. Some of these are directly related to the sexual and reproductive organs, while others have repercussions on other systems of the body and on moods and emotions. This sensitivity to the natural rhythms and changes in the body is called 'fertility awareness' and is the key to success for users of natural methods.

Fertility awareness is not only important in the context of family planning, but also as a general educative process which can help at all life's stages. Teenagers during puberty are undergoing rapid and profound physical, psychological and emotional changes and have great difficulty understanding themselves, let alone being understood by others. An awareness of the developmental processes underlying these changes can go some way towards helping them adjust to their jumbled emotions and live in tune with their bodies.

It can also increase understanding between partners in a sexual relationship. A woman's moods and emotions often spring from the rapidly changing hormonal levels at different times in the cycle. Men are not subject to the same hormonal fluctuations and so generally sail a less stormy sea. An awareness of their different but complementary fertility and sexuality can greatly enhance the quality of the couple's relationship.

Family planning

Natural methods of family planning are based on the biological fact that women are only fertile for a very short time during the menstrual cycle; in other words they are infertile for the greater part of their lives. The aim of all natural methods is to identify this short fertile time in the cycle, so that couples can choose to abstain from sexual intercourse if they wish to avoid a pregnancy or continue sexual activity if they wish to conceive.

This is the second component of natural family planning and involves the practical application of fertility awareness and sexual behaviour in planning the timing and number of children a couple wish to have. This requires a certain skill in selecting and combining indicators to detect as precisely as possible the fertile and infertile phases, and the co-operation of both partners to plan sexual intercourse according to their intentions for a family.

Some couples, if they have chosen natural family planning methods for reasons other than religious ones, may choose to combine fertility observations with effective barrier methods during the fertile time, rather than abstaining from sexual intercourse. However, as this is the fertile time, one proviso against this course of action is that there is an increased risk of pregnancy should the barrier method fail. Also, the use of spermicides interferes with mucus observations.

How effective are natural methods of family planning?

Everyone must have heard the old joke: 'What do you call people who use the rhythm method of birth control?' ANSWER: 'Parents.' Fortunately, natural family planning has progressed a long way since those days. More precise knowledge of how a woman's body works during the menstrual cycle means that some of the modern methods of natural family planning can offer as much protection against an unplanned pregnancy as the contraceptive pill. Dr C. Tietze, a world expert, rates the temperature method (where sexual intercourse is confined to the phase in the cycle after ovulation has occurred) in the top three methods of birth control, together with the pill and sterilisation, in terms of effectiveness and acceptability. The mucus method (which can be used to identify the beginning as well as the end of the fertile phase, thus allowing a couple the chance of intercourse in the phase before ovulation) compares favourably in terms of effectiveness with the sheath or diaphragm. Where more than one indicator is used for identifying the beginning and end of the woman's fertile time, as in the 'multiple-index' methods, this level of effectiveness is further increased and compares well with the effectiveness of the pill.

Obviously, anyone considering natural family planning methods as a way of limiting or spacing their families will want to know how reliable these methods are. In the following chapters, each of the natural methods in use today is looked at in detail, which includes an appraisal of their individual effectiveness.

It should, however, be noted that one of the main problems with studies of the effectiveness of any method of family planning, and particularly natural methods, is how to measure 'success' given the wide variety of factors that can influence the results. In particular, it is important to distinguish between method failure and user failure in accounting for unplanned pregnancies. Method effectiveness refers to the success of the method when it is applied correctly and consistently, i.e. its theoretical effectiveness. For instance, the contraceptive pill has a theoretical effectiveness of almost 100 per cent. The problems arise when the woman forgets to take her pill, or takes it at the wrong time. This is user failure. So, when discussing the success of each natural method in preventing an unplanned pregnancy, figures are given for its effectiveness under ideal conditions and its effectiveness in practice, i.e. when all these other factors are included.

Three factors have been found to have a major influence on the effectiveness of the natural methods. The first factor is the particular natural method used. Table 2 shows the influence of the NFP method used on the pregnancy rates where both the teaching is standardized and the couples are motivated.

One can see that the BBT method has an excellent pregnancy rate equivalent to that of the high-dose combined contraceptive pill or surgical sterilization. One has, however, to realize that the temperature method only detects the post-ovulatory infertile phase so abstinence has to be observed for about two thirds of the cycle which is generally unacceptable to most couples.

Table 2 The importance of choosing an efficient method

Authors and year of publication	Method	No. of couples	Months of exposure	Method Failure				Practice Failure		
				No. of unplanned pregnancies	No. of pregnancies	Failure rate (Pearl)	Success rate%	No. of pregnancies	Failure rate (Pearl)	Success rate%
Marshall 1968	Basal-body temperature (BBT)	351	4,739	–	–	1.2	98.8%	–	5.4	94.6%
World Health Organization 1981	Cervical mucus (Ovulation) method	869	10,215			2.2	97.8%		20%	80%
Frank Hermann et al 1988	Double check method	203	2,630	4	1	0.7	99.3%	4	1.8	98.2%
Barbato et al 1987	Double check method	460	8,140	25	3	0.44	99.5%	22	Teaching error 1.47 User error 1.76	96.32%

Table 3 The importance of efficient teaching

Country	No. of couples	Months of exposure	No. of unplanned pregnancies	Method failure			Practice failure	
				No. of pregnancies	Failure rate (Pearl)	Success rate (%)	No. of pregnancies	Failure rate (Pearl)	Success rate (%)
Canada	125	2651	11	1	0.45	99.5	10	4.53	95.4
France	217	4330	20	2	0.55	99.4	18	4.99	95
Mauritius	184	3813	25	2	0.63	99.4	23	7.24	92.5
USA	114	2226	9	1	0.54	99.5	8	4.31	95.5
Colombia	83	1396	21	3	2.58	97.5	18	15.47	84.5

Note: results from Fairfield Study (1977)

In contrast, the cervical mucus method allows for a more liberal sexual regime in that this indicator can detect both the beginning and the end of the fertile phase. It is also generally considered less laborious than having to take the BBT daily. However, one can see that it is a less efficient method than the BBT. Both method failure and use failure are several times that of the BBT and much higher than current contraceptive methods e.g, the pill and the coil. The newer concept of 'multiple-index methods' was introduced into NFP programmes in 1980 and 1981. After almost a decade of use we now have efficiency surveys which show conclusively that the 'double-check method' has an efficiency rate both for the method and the user efficiency similar to that of the combined pill and sterilization, and better than the minipill and the coil. Intercourse does not have to be restricted to the post-ovulatory phase since this method can detect both the first and last day of the fertile phase with considerable precision and accuracy.

The second factor is the standard of teaching given to a woman or couple about how to use their chosen method. Anyone wishing to use natural methods of family planning should seek advice from specially trained teachers. This is not because the methods are particularly difficult to learn: most women quickly develop an awareness of their own unique pattern of fertility. However, trained counsellors can ensure that the indicators of fertility are being interpreted correctly and the rules of the method properly applied for the purposes of family planning. The correct and consistent use of the method obviously affects its success in preventing a pregnancy.

This book does not aim to provide a self-instruction manual, but to show women and their partners exactly what they can expect and what is involved if they decide to use natural methods, and to back up the teaching supplied by the trained advisers. The addresses of organisations providing advice and teaching in natural methods are given at the end of the book.

The third factor affecting the success of natural methods is the motivation of the couple. The success of all forms of contraception depends very much on how much a couple want to avoid a pregnancy. This is particularly true for natural methods as they require a high degree of commitment, diligence and co-operation from the partners. If they are enthusiastic, determined and well-taught, then the success rates for most natural methods of birth control are at least as good as those for artificial methods of contraception.

The influence of these two factors, teaching and motivation, is apparent in the results acquired by the Fairfield Trial (1977) which studied the effectiveness of the sympto-thermal methods of family planning (see Chapter 6 p.75) in five countries. Table 3 shows the method failure and the user failure rates for each of the countries taking part in the survey. It can be seen from these that Colombia, where there were problems with the training of the teachers, had a failure rate five times higher than the other countries, both for method and user failure.

Table 4   *The importance of motivation of the couple*

Motivation of couple	No. of couples	No. of unplanned pregnancies	Failure rate (Pearl)	Success rate (%)
Well-motivated to prevent a pregnancy	99	2	1.09	99
Less well-motivated, wanting to space children	62	16	16.09	84

Note: results are for Canada, teaching standards equal

Table 4 clearly shows the key role motivation plays in the success or failure of these methods. The results are from the Canadian part of the study and compare the success rates for those couples who wanted to prevent a pregnancy and those who merely intended to space their children. It can be seen that the effectiveness of a method depends largely on how motivated the couple is to use it correctly.

The advantages and disadvantages of natural family planning

The biggest bonus of a natural approach to family planning is its very naturalness: natural methods do not interfere with or interrupt the natural functions of a woman's body in any way and consequently do not pose any threat to her physical health and well-being. Instead, such methods free women from a reliance on devices and drugs and from anxiety about the possibility of harmful side-effects.

In many ways modern artificial methods of birth control have turned a woman's body into a battleground. Natural methods, in contrast, offer women the chance to work, not in opposition to the natural rhythms of their bodies, but in close co-operation with them. To do this involves learning to identify these rhythms – an educative process that is very beneficial in itself. Many woman live in start-ling ignorance of their reproductive system, except for the monthly, often painful, reminders of its functioning. By understanding the processes involved they are much better equipped to cope with what is happening, and for many users of natural methods the feeling of being in tune with their bodies enhances their sense of self-esteem and well-being.

The value of fertility awareness over and above its role in a natural approach to family planning has already been mentioned and will be explored in more detail in Chapter 2. Suffice to repeat here that such knowledge provides a sound foundation for coping with the many potentially disturbing stages of life, from puberty to menopause, by providing an insight into seemingly mystifying physical and psychological reactions.

However, it must be said that natural methods of family planning may not be right for all women. If a woman's lifestyle is such that she has a number of more casual sexual encounters, then the natural methods require the full involvement not only of the woman, but also of her partner: co-operation, caring and commitment between couples are prerequisites for their success. Some restraint from both partners in needed to handle the times when sexual intercourse is prohibited because the woman is in the fertile phase of her cycle (unless the couple have elected to use effective barrier methods at this time), and this is likely to occur only in the context of a mutually supportive relationship.

Surprisingly, couples often report that the appreciation of the sexual element of their relationship is heightened by these periods of abstinence, which encourage them to explore the many other ways of offering a partner love and sexual satisfaction besides penetration. The need for both partners to play an active role in talking about and planning their sexual lives can also promote a deeper understanding and closeness between them. In fact, surveys carried out to canvass opinion among users of natural methods showed that 75 per cent of those interviewed believed that natural family planning had made a positive contribution to their relationships.

It is true that it takes time to learn about natural family planning; it is not an instant answer to the problem of birth control. The first element in the learning process is for the woman (and the man) to gain a sense of her own unique pattern of fertility. Most women achieve this easily and quickly. The second element is to learn how to interpret the different signs of fertility and the rules that should be applied to these interpretations for the purposes of family planning. This can take a little longer, but with the help of specially trained teachers and the support of their partners, women soon become confident in reading their bodily signs and diligently applying the rules of the method. The fact that the methods have to be learned does not mean that natural family planning is only for the clever or well-educated. Rather, all women can be taught to use the methods successfully and women throughout the world, including the less well-developed countries, do just that.

By learning about all the indicators of fertility and their expression in the body, a woman can decide which are best suited to her unique hormonal pattern. In the following chapters the advantages and drawbacks of the several indicators are highlighted and alternatives or combinations proposed so that the reader can make an informed decision for herself. In this way the method can be tailored to the requirements of each individual woman.

A common criticism levelled at natural methods is that they are the only suitable for women with regular cycles. On the contrary, as each woman can determine which indicators are the easiest and most reliable for her and then chart them every day of her cycle, any irregularities will show up on the chart and can be accommodated accordingly.

Whichever indicator or combination of indicators is selected, it is vital that these are observed every day without fail and the information gathered recorded on the special fertility charts, and the rules of the method diligently and consistently applied if an unplanned pregnancy is to be avoided. On first sight the daily observations and all the form-filling may seem a chore but most women report that this quickly becomes second nature to them.

As a truly positive approach to family planning, natural methods not only work in preventing a pregnancy, but can also be used to maximise the chances of conception. For those couples experiencing difficulties with conception, learning about fertility awareness and how to pinpoint the most fertile time in the woman's cycle can be of invaluable assistance.

As with all methods of birth control, natural family planning has advantages and disadvantages; it will be totally unacceptable to some couples and the perfect way to handle birth control for others. Certainly, those couples who elect to use natural methods find that the advantages of a reliable method without adverse side-effects considerably outweigh any inconvenience caused by the routine of daily charting or periodic abstinence. The most important point to remember when considering natural family planning is that it is not so much a technique as a way of life.

Selecting a method of family planning

No method of birth control, artificial or natural, is best for everyone. Many factors have to be considered when choosing a birth control method, and the aim of this book is to provide the information necessary for a woman and her partner to make an informed decision about this very important part of their lives, with particular emphasis on the natural methods of family planning that are available.

Listed below are just some of the questions that you should bear in mind when selecting any method of family planning, whether natural or artificial.

- What is your general state of health?
- How old are you?
- What medical care is available to you?
- Do you want to prevent a pregnancy, or just postpone it because you want to space your family?
- How acceptable is the method to you? Will you feel comfortable using it? (The more acceptable the method, the more likely it is that you will apply it consistently and correctly, and therefore the greater its chance of successfully avoiding a pregnancy.)
- Does it fit in with your religious and cultural beliefs? (If not, it could give rise to feelings of guilt and anxiety which could undermine your sexual relationship.)
- What type of sexual relationship(s) do you have? Do you need birth control as part of a long-term committed relationship, or for more numerous casual encounters?
- How often do you have intercourse? (Everybody has different levels of sexual need.)
- Does the method involve any potential risk to your health? Are there any side-effects to take into consideration?
- Is contraception up to you alone, or can you discuss sex and birth control freely and openly with your partner? Is he prepared to be co-operative and supportive on this issue?

- How would you feel if your chosen method of birth control failed and you became pregnant?

Thinking through these questions will help you determine exactly what you need in terms of birth control and which method would best meet your specific requirements. Some of the answers may well encourage you to inquire further into whether one of the natural methods of family planning might not fulfil your requirements. Hopefully, this book will help you to answer that question.

2

Our bodies

Natural family planning is not just a set of rules for avoiding or achieving pregnancy. It involves a real understanding of the natural processes of the body that result in fertility, and the close observation of the body's own signs and signals of this fertility. The first step in successfully applying the methods of natural family planning is to learn how our bodies work.

Basically, to be fertile you need
> a living sperm (in the man)
> a living egg or ovum (in the woman)

The lifespan of an ovum, from the moment it is released from the ovary to its disintegration if unfertilised, is relatively short – about 12–24 hours. So, in every cycle the period of a woman's fertility is very brief. As a woman is infertile until puberty and then again after the menopause, it has been estimated that she is only fertile for about 4 per cent of her life.

On the other hand, once he has passed puberty, a man is potentially fertile well into old age. Every time a man ejaculates he releases millions of sperm that can survive in a woman's body for as long as three to five days. It is important, therefore, to consider the fertility of both woman and man.

With this in mind, we need to consider the man's reproductive system and how sperm are produced.

The man's reproductive system

A young boy is infertile until puberty, when several physical changes occur, the most striking being the growth and development of his sex organs which also begin to function at this time.

The primary male reproductive glands are the two oval-shaped testicles or *testes*. These have two functions: (1) to produce sperm, and (2) to secrete the male sex hormones (androgens), the most important of which is testosterone. It is this hormone that is responsible for the development of the secondary sex characteristics, such as the growth of facial and body hair, deepening of the voice, and muscular and bone development.

The testes are held in a soft muscular pouch called the *scrotum*, which hangs outside the body. This means that the testes are at a slightly lower temperature than the rest of the body. As sperm require a temperature a degree or two below normal body temperature, the scrotum provides the ideal environment for sperm production.

Inside, each testis is divided into approximately 300 compartments, each one containing tightly coiled tubules, known as the *seminiferous tubules*. These are lined with rapidly dividing cells which produce the sperm.

The hundreds of sperm-producing tubules join together to form ducts which act as passage-ways for the sperm, leading into a single tube on the surface of each testis, called the *epididymis*. Here the sperm are stored while they undergo a complex process of maturation. Each epididymis, in turn, leads into a muscular sperm duct or *vas deferens*. The two ducts (one from each testis) pass into the abdomen and up over the bladder. If a man has a vasectomy, these sperm ducts are cut and tied so that the sperm are unable to leave the testes.

The sperm ducts from each side open into the *urethra*, the tube which runs from the bladder through the length of the *penis* to the outside. The urethra plays two roles: it allows urine to pass from the bladder to the outside, and, when the penis is erect, it allows sperm to be ejaculated. There is a small circular muscle at the base of the bladder which contracts when a man ejaculates so that urine cannot enter the urethra at the same time as the sperm.

The sperm are carried in seminal fluid composed of secretions from the two *seminal vesicles*, the *prostate gland* and *Cowper's gland* (the position of these organs is shown in Figure 1). These secretions provide nourishment for the sperm and a medium for swimming when the sperm enter the woman's vagina. The fluid from the prostate gland enables the sperm to move properly, while the secretions from the seminal vesicles provide a slightly alkaline environment which protects the sperm from the natural acidity of the woman's vaginal secretions.

The sensitive tip of the penis, the *glans*, is covered by a loose hood of skin known as the foreskin. A part of the foreskin is removed when a man is circumcised. The shaft of the penis is made up of soft, spongy tissue which, when the man is sexually aroused, fills with blood to become firm so that sexual intercourse can take place.

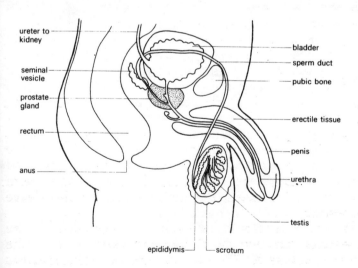

Figure 1   Cross-section of the man's reproductive system

The sperm

From puberty sperm are constantly produced in a man's testes. It is hard to imagine, but a healthy man produces about 50,000 sperm a minute, or 72 million a day. In general it takes a sperm 60–72 days to grow to maturity. If they are not ejaculated, the sperm simply break down and are absorbed back into the system. Individual sperm are minute and can only be seen through a microscope. Each one consists of three parts: a head, a neck and a tail (see Figure 2). The head contains the genetic package of chromosomes, the man's contribution to the heredity of his child; the neck contains the energy system that nourishes the sperm and helps them move; the tail is the motor, propelling the sperm forward by lashing from side to side, thus enabling the sperm to 'swim' up the woman's vagina to the uterus and on up the fallopian tubes in search of a mature ovum.

Figure 2 Sperm

When a man ejaculates the semen (the sperm combined with the fluids from the other sex glands) is forced out through the urethra in spurts by the rhythmic contractions of the epididymis, the sperm ducts and other muscles in the region. Each ejaculation contains between 300 and 600 million sperm, but only a single sperm is required to fertilise the ovum.

The woman's reproductive system

Whereas a young boy does not start to produce sperm until puberty, a baby girl is born with several thousand partly developed egg cells or ova in her ovaries – enough for a lifetime. No new ova are produced after birth. The ova lie dormant until the girl reaches puberty, somewhere between the ages of 10 and 15 years. After puberty the ova are released one at a time about every four weeks, although the length of the cycle varies from woman to woman. Unlike a man, a woman is only fertile when the ovum has been released: in other words, her fertility is cyclical. Nor is she fertile for the remainder of her life, as are men, but only until the menopause which occurs around 40–50 years of age.

The external genitals (Figure 3)

These are the parts of the genitals outside the body, which the woman can see for herself with the help of a mirror. They are collectively termed the *vulva*. They include two thick folds of skin called the *labia*, or the lips of the vagina. The large outer folds are the *labia majora*, which join at the top at the *mons pubis*, the soft mound that becomes covered in pubic hair after puberty. The smaller inner lips on each side of the vaginal opening are referred to as the *labia minora*. These join just below the mons pubis to form a soft fold of skin which encircles the *clitoris*. This is the most sensitive spot in the female genitals and is composed of erectile tissue, similar to that in the man's penis, which swells when the woman is sexually aroused. Hidden by the

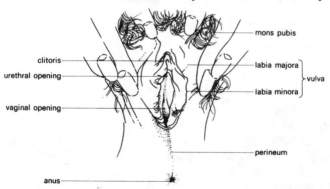

Figure 3 The woman's external genitals

labia minora, the *urethra* from the bladder opens just below the clitoris in the area known as the *vestibule*. Behind the vulva is the anus and the area between the anus and the vulva is called the perineum.

The internal genitals (Figure 4)

Just inside the opening of the vagina is a crescent-shaped piece of thin tissue called the *hymen* which partially blocks the opening. The shape and size of the hymen vary from woman to woman. It can be broken the first time the woman has sexual intercourse, or it may be torn earlier by exercise, sports or the insertion of tampons. Many women do not even notice when the hymen is first torn.

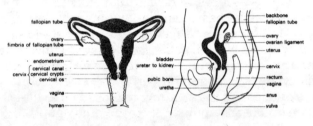

Figure 4a and 4b   The woman's reproductive system

The *vagina* is a cylindrical passage leading from the vulva to the internal genitals. Its walls are lined by a soft mucous membrane in which there are folds or wrinkles called ruggae. The walls of the vagina may be almost dry to very wet, depending on the stage in the menstrual cycle. The secretions from the mucous membrane provide lubrication and protect the vagina from infection. On either side of the vaginal opening are two small glands, Bartholin's glands, which secrete a small amount of fluid in response to sexual stimulation.

Just before the end of the vagina, or *fornix*, is the *cervix* (the neck of the womb). This is a muscular canal about 2 cm long, the top end of which opens into the womb and the lower end into the vagina. The lower opening can be felt by inserting a finger gently into the vagina. It feels to the touch like the tip of a nose or a small chin with a dimple. The dimple is the *cervical os*, a tiny opening about the diameter of a thin straw. The width of the os and the position and texture of the cervix change around the time of ovulation. These changes can be detected by the woman herself and used as a guide to her fertile phase (see pages 71–77).

The cervical canal is lined with *cervical crypts* which produce a fluid called *cervical mucus*, vital for the survival and movement of the man's sperm. The mucus varies in appearance and texture as a consequence of the changing levels of hormones during the menstrual cycle. In the early part of the cycle the mucus is whitish, thick and sticky, but as ovulation approaches it becomes clear, thin and slippery – rather like raw egg-white – to assist the passage of the sperm into the fallopian tubes so fertilisation can take place.

Once ovulation has occurred, the mucus decreases in quantity and becomes thicker. Women who decide to use natural methods of family planning are taught how to 'read' their mucus as an indicator of the fertile and infertile phases of their cycles (see pages 55–70).

The upper end of the cervical canal opens into the womb or *uterus*. In a woman who is not pregnant the uterus is about the size of a fist and similar in shape to an upside-down pear (see Figure 5). The uterus has thick walls made of one of the most powerful muscles in the body. It is here that the baby grows and is nourished during the nine months of pregnancy until birth. The uterus is lined by a special layer of cells called the *endometrium*, which thickens every month to provide a 'nesting place' for the fertilised ovum at the earliest moments of pregnancy. If conception does not take place, this lining is not required; it then disintegrates and is passed out of the body as the menstrual flow or period.

Extending from the upper end of the uterus are two tubes, the *fallopian tubes*. About 10 cm long, these are the passageways from the ovaries to the uterus and look a little like ram's horns. The lower end of the tube at the uterus has a very narrow opening; the other end is funnel-shaped and fringed with fingerlike projections called *fimbria*. The fallopian tubes are not attached to the ovaries but surround

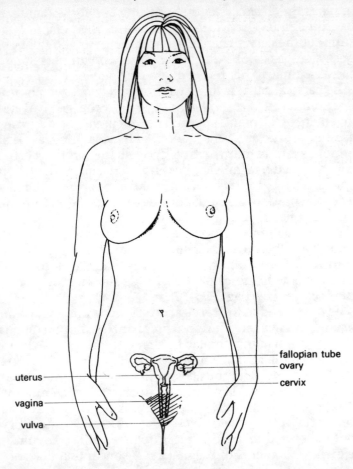

Figure 5 The position of the woman's reproductive organs

and envelop them at the upper end. When an ovum is released from the ovary it is drawn into the fallopian tube by the movement of the fimbria and propelled down the tube. If the ovum meets a sperm while in the tube, fertilisation occurs.

The primary female reproductive glands are the *ovaries*, of which there are two positioned on either side of the upper part of the uterus. These are not directly connected to the uterus or the fallopian tubes but are held in place by fibrous folds of tissue known as *ovarian ligaments*. The ovaries have two important functions: (1) to produce ova, and (2) to secrete the hormones oestrogen and progesterone. Within the ovary the immature ova are contained in protective cavities called *follicles* and every cycle, from puberty to the menopause, one of these follicles ripens under the influence of the hormones and releases an ovum (Figure 6) into the fallopian tube. This process is called *ovulation* and will be discussed in more detail later in this chapter (see pages 29–30).

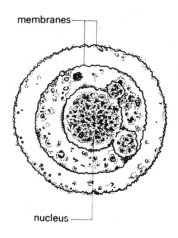

membranes

nucleus

Figure 6 An ovum

The breasts
One of the first signs of sexual development in a young girl is the change in her breasts as the ovaries start to secrete hormones at the onset of puberty. The breasts are made up of milk-producing glands surrounded by fatty tissue which gives the breast its shape. When a woman is breast feeding, milk is conveyed along milk ducts which open in and around the nipple. The breast tissue is very responsive to changes in hormonal levels during the menstrual cycle

and many women notice changes in the size and shape of their breasts as their cycles progress. These changes can be useful as 'extra' signals of the body's natural rhythms.

The menstrual cycle
The menstrual cycle is controlled by the complex interplay of hormones (the chemical messengers of the body) and the reproductive organs, which ensures that each month an ovum is released from the ovaries at just the right time for possible fertilisation by a sperm (Figure 7). Four hormones are involved: follicle stimulating hormone (FSH) and luteinising hormone (LH) which are produced by the pituitary gland (located near the base of the brain, above the roof of the mouth), and oestrogen and progesterone produced by the ovaries.

The length of the menstrual cycle varies from woman to woman. Some women have short cycles – 23 days or less, others have long cycles – over 35 days, while the average length is 28–30 days. Very few women have an absolutely regular menstrual cycle and a few days either way is considered perfectly normal. Whatever its length, a woman is only fertile for a few days within that cycle. Also, for individual

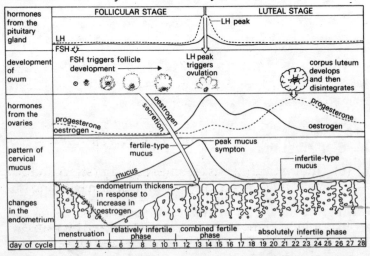

Figure 7 The complex feedback system of the menstrual cycle

28

women the time from ovulation to menstruation is usually very regular.

What happens during the menstrual cycle?

1 The cycle begins when the pituitary gland releases FSH into the bloodstream. This triggers the development of three or four follicles containing the immature ova in the ovaries, hence the term 'follicular phase' (see Figure 8).

2 As the follicles develop one (or occasionally two) becomes dominant, while the others regress. This dominant follicle secretes greater and greater amounts of oestrogen. The rising level of oestrogen in the bloodstream has three effects:

   (a) less FSH is produced in order to inhibit the development of any more ova;

   (b) the lining of the uterus starts to thicken in readiness to receive the fertilised ovum;

   (c) the glands in the cervix start to produce mucus that is favourable to the survival of the sperm.

3 As the ovum continues to ripen the oestrogen level reaches a peak, and this triggers the pituitary gland to start releasing LH.

4 LH flows into the bloodstream and causes the follicle to rupture, releasing the ovum into the fallopian tube. This is *ovulation*.

5 The empty follicle forms the corpus luteum (hence the 'luteal phase'), or yellow body, which starts to secrete progesterone. When this happens:

   (a) the pituitary gland is prevented from producing LH or FSH, so ovulation cannot occur again in this cycle;

   (b) the cervical mucus becomes thick and sticky and acts as a 'plug' in the cervix to stop sperm entering the uterus.

6 If the ovum in the fallopian tube is fertilised by a sperm, it travels down the tube to the uterus and embeds itself in the prepared endometrium (Figure 8). The corpus

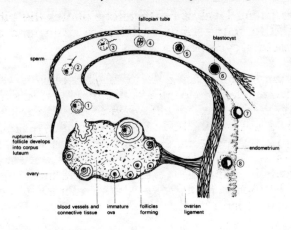

Figure 8   Ovulation, fertilisation and implantation

1 A mature ovum is released from a follicle in the ovary: this is the moment of *ovulation*. The ovum is 'caught' by the fimbria of the fallopian tube and swept along the tube towards the uterus.

2 One of the sperm travelling up the tube from the vagina and uterus successfully penetrates the outer membrane of the ovum.

3 The nucleus of the sperm and the nucleus of the ovum fuse together. This is *fertilisation*.

4, 5, and 6 The fertilised ovum continues its journey along the fallopian tube. As it does so, the single cell divides and multiplies to produce a 'blastocyst' – the complete blueprint for the new life.

7 The blastocyst starts to burrow its way into the prepared lining of the uterus, until

8 it is completely *implanted* in the endometrium. The process from fertilisation to implantation takes several days.

    luteum continues to secrete progesterone throughout the early stages of the pregnancy.

7   If the ovum is not fertilised, it still travels down the fallopian tube to the uterus, but is then shed. The corpus luteum starts to disintegrate and stops producing progesterone. As the levels of progesterone fall, the endometrium breaks up and is passed out of the body. This is *menstruation*.

8   The falling level of progesterone allows the pituitary gland to start secreting FSH once again, and a new menstrual cycle begins.

This complex feedback system of hormones is affected when women take the contraceptive pill. Most pills contain some form of oestrogen and progesterone which keep the hormonal levels of the body artificially high. This prevents the pituitary gland from releasing FSH or LH and so ovulation is suppressed. The thickening of the endometrium still occurs in response to the oestrogen in the pill. When the pill is stopped for a few days, the endometrium breaks down as usual and 'menstruation' occurs.

3

The fertility cycle

A woman's menstrual cycle could also be described as her cycle of fertility. Each menstrual cycle her body is prepared for the release of a ripe ovum and for the possibility of conception. Natural methods of family planning depend

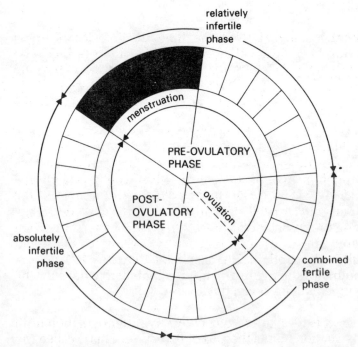

relatively
infertile
phase

menstruation

PRE-OVULATORY
PHASE

ovulation

POST-
OVULATORY
PHASE

absolutely
infertile
phase

combined
fertile
phase

Figure 9 The fertility cycle

upon the woman getting to know her own unique cycle of fertility so that she can assess which are the fertile and infertile times.

When is the fertile phase?

The fertility cycle can be divided into three phases (Figure 9):

Phase 1   covers the period from menstruation to the time when the follicles start maturing in the ovaries. As this part of the cycle varies from cycle to cycle for individual women as well as from woman to woman, it is the most problematic in terms of making accurate assessments of fertility. For this reason it is referred to as the *relatively infertile phase*.

Phase 2   extends from the time the follicles begin to develop to 48 hours after ovulation has occurred. (The 48 hours allows 24 hours for the lifespan of the ovum and 24 hours as a safety margin, because it is impossible to be precise about the actual time of ovulation.) This is the *fertile phase*.

A woman is only fertile after ovulation has taken place, and then only for the brief lifespan of the ovum. However, to this has to be added the fertility of her partner and the potential lifespan of the sperm, which can survive in the woman's system for up to five days with the help of the cervical mucus produced during this phase of the cycle. Taking the combined fertility of the two partners, there are several days in each cycle when sexual intercourse could result in conception. The *combined fertile phase* is therefore 48 hours for the ovum and approximately five days for the sperm, equalling seven days.

Phase 3   is measured from a few days after ovulation until menstruation marks the end of that cycle. This is called the *absolutely infertile phase* in contrast to the relatively infer-

33

tile phase. Most women find that the length of this phase of the cycle is fairly consistent from cycle to cycle and lasts for approximately 10–16 days (see Figure 10). Once ovulation has occurred the hormone levels rise rapidly to prevent the possibility of a second ovulation in that cycle. Thus, fertilisation is impossible during this phase. (Non-identical twins occur when two ova are released in one cycle, but both ova have to be released in quick succession. Identical twins are the result of one ovum splitting in two after it has been fertilised.)

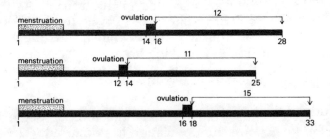

Figure 10 The time span from ovulation to menstruation is usually regular for individual women

How do you know when you are in the fertile phase?

Natural family planning would be a wonderfully simple exercise if women released a ripe ovum at exactly the same time in each cycle. Unfortunately, this process is never so clear-cut and even women whose menstrual cycles are normally regular note irregularities from time to time, all of which affect the timing of the fertile phase.

However, a woman's body does produce 'signals', or clues to what is happening. As the fertility cycle runs its course the hormones oestrogen and progesterone affect the body in various ways. The woman is not aware of many of these effects, but she can detect some of the bodily changes that occur and learn to recognise and interpret them as indicators of the different phases of her cycle.

The major observable indicators of the fertility cycle are:

1   Changes in the basal body temperature.
2   Changes in the quantity and quality of the mucus pro-
    duced by the cervix.
3   Changes in the cervix itself.

There are also a host of minor indicators, such as breast tenderness, ovulation pain, changes of mood and so on, which vary from woman to woman. Once the woman has been alerted to these signals, they can become useful back-up indicators of the different phases.

How are the indicators of fertility used?

A study of the fertility cycle shows that if it were possible to detect the first and last days of the fertile phase, the relatively infertile phase and the absolutely infertile phase would fall into place. All methods of natural family planning are aimed at determining, as accurately as poss-ible, the beginning and end of the fertile phase. The choice of indicator or indicators for detecting the fertile phase determines the method of family planning. Traditionally, three main methods of natural family planning are in common use.

1   The temperature method
The indicator in this method is the sudden rise in the woman's basal body temperature that occurs around the time of ovulation. From this it is possible to calculate the end of the fertile phase and the beginning of the absolutely infertile phase. It does not, however, enable us to detect the beginning of the fertile phase.

2   The cervical mucus method (also known as the Billings method and the ovulation method)

The production of mucus in the cervix is directly controlled by the levels of hormones at various stages in the fertility cycle. When ovulation is imminent the hormonal activity causes the cervix to manufacture a thin, watery mucus designed to assist the passage of the sperm to the waiting ovum. Once ovulation has occurred a change in hormonal activity causes the cervix to produce a thick sticky mucus which literally plugs the opening of the uterus to prevent sperm entering. These changes in the pattern of mucus production indicate the onset and end of the fertile phase.

3 The symptothermal method

As the title suggests this method involves taking the changes in the basal body temperature as the major indicator and combining it with observation of one or more of the other indicators of fertility. Using this method it is possible to determine the beginning and end of the fertile phase.

Multiple-index methods

Practical experience suggests that this traditional division of methods is often too rigid and confining when applied to individual situations. Instead, we have developed a more flexible, woman-oriented approach to natural family planning, which allows the individual woman scope in determining what method is best for her, given her specific requirements.

This approach has a broader framework and subdivides the natural methods into the following:

1 Single-index methods – in which only one indicator of the different phases of the cycle is used.
2 Multiple-index methods – in which several indicators are used in combination. This differs from the symptothermal method, to which it is closely related, in that temperature need not necessarily be one of the indicators used.

The fertility cycle

Each woman has a unique pattern of hormone production. The effect of these hormones on specific organs is also unique to the individual, as, consequently, are her predominant signs and symptoms of fertility. The art of successful natural family planning is for each woman to discover which are her best indicators of fertility, and so tailor the method to suit her requirements. At first a woman may want to use several indicators to assess the fertile phase of the cycle; as she gets to know her body and gains confidence in reading the signs of her fertility, she may find that a single indicator is sufficient. In either case she is free to choose the methods in which she and her partner have most confidence.

The next step is to examine in detail the major indicators of fertility to see how each can best be observed in the body, how their individual patterns can be charted and what rules apply to their interpretation, taken either singly or in combination.

4

The temperature method

Immediately after ovulation has occurred the increase in the progesterone secreted by the corpus luteum causes a woman's basal body temperature (BBT) to rise by several points of a degree. (Basal body temperature is the temperature of the body at rest.) Her temperature will remain at this higher level until a day or two before menstruation. This pattern of a low temperature for the first part of the cycle and a higher temperature for the second part is known as a biphasic pattern and can be observed easily if an accurate record of daily temperatures is maintained throughout the cycle.

The shift in temperature indicates that ovulation has taken place for that cycle, so, allowing for the survival time of the ovum, the woman is now in the absolutely infertile phase and conception will not be possible for the rest of that cycle. (This method does not reveal anything about the potential fertility of the days preceding ovulation.)

The equipment you will need

As the temperature changes you are trying to record are really quite small – only about 0.2°C (0.35°F) – it is best to use a special fertility thermometer. This is calibrated in tenths of a degree and only covers the range 35°C–39°C (95°F–102°F), making it more accurate and easier to read than a normal clinical thermometer.

The daily readings are recorded on a special temperature chart designed for the purpose. Both the thermometer and the chart are available from the National Association of NFP Teachers, natural family planning clinics or your own general practitioner. The clinic will also instruct you fully on the use of temperature as a method of family planning.

How to measure your basal body temperature

1   Always take your temperature *before* getting up in the morning. BBT is the temperature of the body at rest, and as soon as you start moving around, eating or drinking, your body temperature rises. (If you are working on night shifts, you should take your temperature in the evening after rest.)
2   Take your temperature as near as possible to the same time each day. The BBT fluctuates in a cyclical pattern throughout the day and night, the lowest point being in the early hours of the morning and rising about 0.1°C (0.2°F) every hour after that time. If you take your temperature an hour or more earlier or later than usual, this will obviously affect the reading.
3   BBT can be measured orally, vaginally or rectally. As the temperature in the vagina and rectum is a little higher than in the mouth, it is important to stick to whichever method you have chosen for the entire cycle. Check that the thermometer reading is 35°C (95°F) before using it. If taking your temperature orally, place the thermometer under your tongue and leave it in place for at least 5 minutes. If taking your temperature vaginally or rectally, insert the thermometer gently into your vagina or rectum, not too deeply, and leave for at least 3 minutes.
4   Remove the thermometer and read the temperature. Record this reading on the chart. (Instructions on how to complete the charts are provided below.)

5   Rinse the thermometer clean, using cool water (hot water may break the mercury column), and return it to its usual storage place.

Tips

1   Keep the thermometer within easy reach of the bed.
2   Shake the thermometer down the night before, or better still, ask your partner to do it as a sign of the shared responsibility.
3   If occasionally you feel too groggy in the morning to fill in your chart immediately, you can take your temperature and then put the thermometer in a safe place to read and record the information later in the day. Providing you do not put the thermometer near a radiator or somewhere where it might get knocked to the floor, the mercury in the column will not change.
4   Use the same thermometer for the entire cycle. If you do have to change it because of breakage or loss, be sure to mark the day you start using the new thermometer on your chart to avoid any confusion from false temperature increases that are a consequence of the new thermometer.
5   Keep a spare thermometer in stock. It is easy to forget to buy a new one if you should lose or break the one you are using, and this would interrupt the temperature taking and confuse the pattern for that cycle.

How to chart your BBT

Use the special fertility temperature chart, an example of which is shown in Chart 1. The calendar date is written at the top of the chart, while the days of the cycle are shown at the bottom. Day 1 of the fertility cycle is taken as the first day of menstrual bleeding. The temperature is printed in both centigrade and fahrenheit on the vertical axis on the left of the chart.

At the bottom of the chart is a line entitled 'disturbances'. Here you should note anything that might have caused a rise in your temperature. Some common causes of disturbances to the BBT are listed later in this chapter.

To mark the reading for the day, find the day of the cycle, then the temperature you have recorded that morning, and put a dot in the appropriate square. As the cycle progresses, join up the dots so that you can see at a glance the changes in the BBT pattern.

How to read the temperature chart

Chart 1 is a typical temperature chart for one cycle. It shows two distinct phases: a low phase in the first part of the cycle and high phase in the second part. The two phases are divided by the temperature shift, which in this chart measures 0.2°C (0.35°F) and occurs between days 15 and 16. The reading taken as the first high temperature (in this case that on day 16) must be higher than all the low temperatures and must be preceded by not less than six low temperature readings. To ensure that it is a genuine temperature shift and not a one-off increase, this higher temperature must be sustained for three consecutive days.

The temperature shift is recognised more easily if a horizontal line – a coverline – is drawn over the low phase temperatures. In Chart 1 the coverline is drawn between 36.55°C (97.8°F) and 36.60°C (97.9°F), showing clearly that the temperatures for days 16, 17 and 18 are all above the coverline and therefore above the low phase temperatures.

Occasionally, the temperature chart shows a drop in the BBT just before the temperature shift occurs. It is believed that this is caused by the drop in oestrogen level which occurs at or just before ovulation. However, this only happens for a few women.

The low BBT in the first phase of the cycle is maintained by the hormone oestrogen. The temperature shift and subsequent high BBT in the second phase is caused by the increase in progesterone released by the corpus luteum after ovulation. Once the temperature has been sustained at the high level for 48 hours, which is recognised by the three consecutive daily readings, it can be assumed that ovulation has taken place and that the ovum, if not fertilised, has died. This means that you are now in the absolutely infertile phase of the cycle and conception cannot occur for the remainder of that cycle. If the temperature method is used alone as a single-index method of natural family planning, a couple who do not wish to conceive must avoid sexual intercourse until the morning of the third day after the temperature shift, which in Chart 1 would be day 18.

Disturbances to the BBT

There can be several reasons for 'false' rises in temperature readings, but some of the commonest ones are listed here:

1   Taking your temperature at a different time from usual. As many women tend to take their temperatures later at weekends than the rest of the week, these disturbed readings are referred to as the 'weekend syndrome'.
2   A late night can affect the temperature in the morning, as can a glass or two of alcohol.
3   Illness, such as a sore throat or a cold. However, increases in temperature as a result of a fever would create an enormous peak on this chart as it registers such small changes in temperature, so there should be no risk of confusing temperature rises caused by illness with those caused by the occurrence of ovulation.
4   A disturbed night's sleep, such as getting up for children.
5   Shift work.
6   Changes in environment, for example, going away on holiday.
7   Stress.

It is important to recognise the possibility of disturbance to the BBT and mark it on your chart. In this way, sudden rises in temperature disturbing the low phase temperatures can be excluded, so that the biphasic pattern is

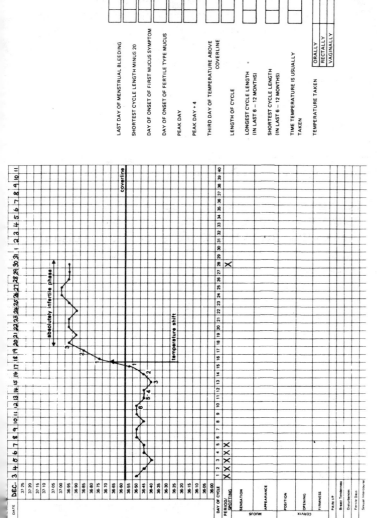

Chart 1 A typical basal body temperature (BBT) chart.

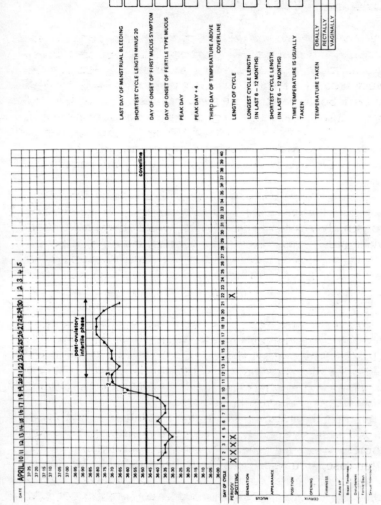

LAST DAY OF MENSTRUAL BLEEDING

SHORTEST CYCLE LENGTH MINUS 20

DAY OF ONSET OF FIRST MUCUS SYMPTOM

DAY OF ONSET OF FERTILE TYPE MUCUS

PEAK DAY

PEAK DAY + 4

THIRD DAY OF TEMPERATURE ABOVE COVERLINE

LENGTH OF CYCLE

LONGEST CYCLE LENGTH (IN LAST 6 – 12 MONTHS)

SHORTEST CYCLE LENGTH (IN LAST 6 – 12 MONTHS)

TIME TEMPERATURE IS USUALLY TAKEN

TEMPERATURE TAKEN

	ORALLY
	RECTALLY
	VAGINALLY

Chart 2 The BBT readings for a short cycle.

discernible and you are not misled into thinking that ovulation has occurred before it really has.

Variations in BBT patterns

The charts shown in this chapter illustrate some of the possible variations in BBT patterns. Although we talk of a 'typical' chart, this description is not entirely accurate. As every woman's fertility cycle is unique, so also is her BBT pattern. Some patterns are more common than others, but those described as less 'typical' are in no way abnormal, unless they indicate a definite fertility problem, such as a complete lack of ovulation. Charting the BBT for a few cycles will quickly reveal what is a typical pattern for you.

Chart 2 shows the BBT pattern for a woman whose cycles are relatively short – in this example, 21 days. Some women always have short cycles, while others have short cycles only occasionally. This woman knows that her cycles are regular but short and so has started recording her BBT before her period has finished. The temperature shift is easily discernible: the temperatures for days 10, 11 and 12 are all above the coverline and the rise in temperature is sustained for three consecutive days. The absolutely infertile phase begins on the morning of the third day after the temperature shift, which is day 12 in this cycle. Although the whole cycle is short, this last phase is within the limits of a normal cycle (10–16 days) and menstruation starts about 12 days after ovulation.

In contrast, Chart 3 illustrates a relatively long cycle. As for short cycles, long cycles are customary for some women, while for others they occur occasionally. In the latter case, ovulation may have been delayed by illness or some emotional disturbance. The temperature shift is still evident, but it indicates that ovulation did not take place until about day 20. The infertile phase after ovulation therefore starts on day 23 – the third day of a sustained temperature increase after an obvious low phase.

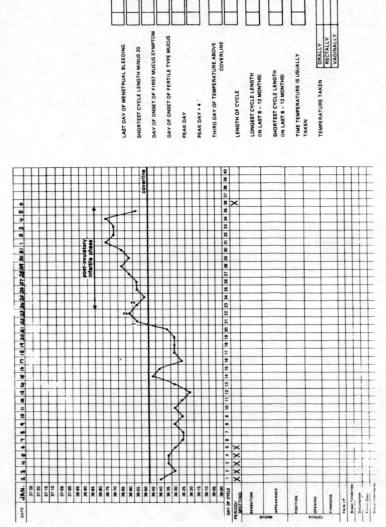

Chart 3 The BBT readings for a long cycle.

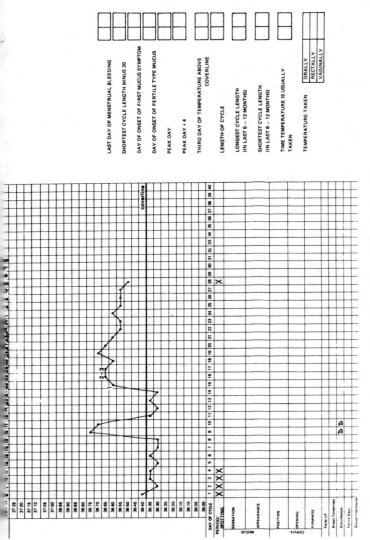

Chart 4   The effect of alcohol on BBT readings.

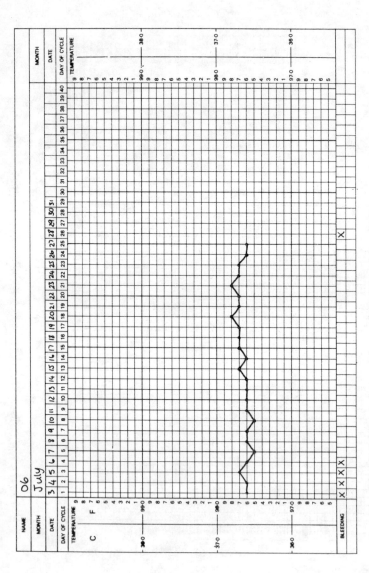

Chart 5 A poorly designed chart: is this cycle anovulatory?

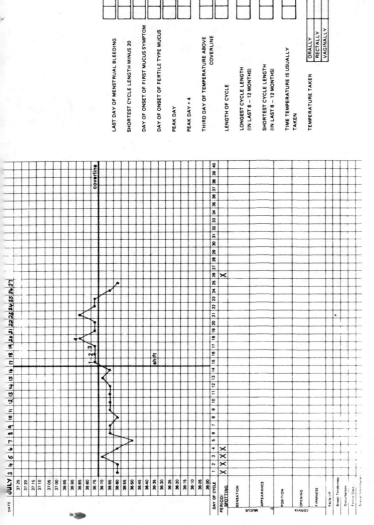

Chart 6 A properly designed chart: the temperature shift is now quite clear.

For the woman who is expecting a long cycle in line with her normal cycle lengths of 35 days or more, the fact that ovulation did not occur until about the twentieth day will not have been a surprise, and she and her partner would have been able to plan their sexual relations accordingly.

However, if the woman normally has regular cycles of shorter duration and suddenly experiences a long cycle such as this one, there is a danger that she will be over-eager to see a temperature rise and so misinterpret the temperature readings. If the woman who completed Chart 3 normally had cycles of about 28 days, she may have been tempted to interpret the increase in temperature on days 14 and 15 as a temperature shift, and may have had sexual intercourse just when she was at the peak of her fertility. However, the temperatures on days 14 and 15 are not significantly above the previous low temperatures, nor was the rise maintained over three consecutive days, indicating that it was not a true temperature shift. The temperature increase evident on days 21, 22 and 23 does comply with the rules for identifying a true temperature shift. This shows the importance of diligent, accurate temperature recording and careful interpretation of the information. If in doubt, wait for the situation to clarify itself (as it did in this chart), or there is the risk of an unplanned pregnancy.

It is also important to make a note of any possible disturbances to the BBT readings, otherwise 'false' increases in temperature may confuse the interpretation. Note the high temperature readings for days 9 and 10 in Chart 4. These readings coincided with a weekend, during which the woman had enjoyed a few glasses of wine on both evenings and a longer 'lie-in' than usual, resulting in a considerable increase in the BBT reading on the following mornings. Realising the cause, she could disregard this increase in interpreting the chart.

Be careful to use the correct charts for recording the BBT pattern as this can affect the 'readability' of the chart. Ideally, each little box on the graph should be a square rather than a rectangle. The temperature graph in Chart

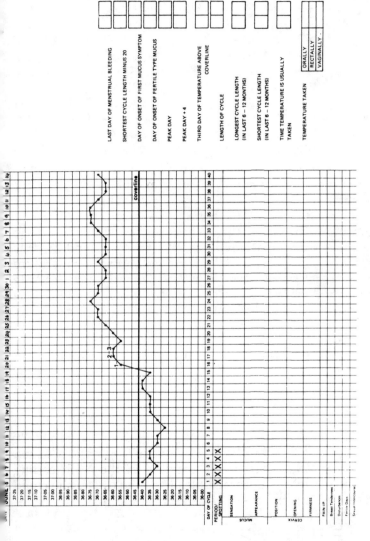

Chart 7 A cycle during which pregnancy is achieved.

5, for example, appears to show a cycle with no temperature shift and therefore, presumably, no ovulation. Yet an
obvious temperature shift can be seen if these readings are
transferred to a properly designed chart (see Chart 6). Note
that in this particular case it was necessary to wait an extra
day to reach a temperature reading that was 0.2°C (0.35°F)
above the last low temperature reading before ovulation.

In a normal cycle, if the ovum is not fertilised, the high
temperature phase following ovulation continues until a
day or two before the next menstruation, when it drops
noticeably in response to the decrease in progesterone as
the corpus luteum comes to the end of its life. However,
if the ovum released during that cycle is fertilised, the
progesterone levels stay high for three months and so
do the BBT readings. In fact, one of the earliest signs of
pregnancy is a rise in the BBT after ovulation which lasts
for 20 days or more (see Chart 7).

Finally, not all temperature shifts follow a straight-
forward pattern. Some go up in a zig-zag manner, while
others rise slowly or increase in steps. In these cases the
advice of an NFP teacher can be invaluable in showing
how such charts should be interpreted, either for avoiding
a pregnancy or in helping to achieve one.

The advantages and disadvantages of the temperature method

One advantage of the temperature chart is that it is an
objective indicator of fertility. It can be examined and
interpreted by teachers and others. Men often report that
they become co-partners in the temperature charting,
which gives them a greater awareness of shared fertility
than when the woman only keeps a record of other fertility
indicators. Indeed, many male partners like to take the
responsibility for temperature charting and interpretation.

Because of its objectivity, the temperature method is often very helpful for women beginning to learn to observe
other indicators of fertility such as the cervical mucus

pattern and changes in the cervix. It takes some time for women to master these latter indicators and to use them either singly or in combination. Recognising the temperature shift can help to overcome any doubts and difficulties during the learning phase.

In certain women who have a hormonal imbalance producing erratic patches of mucus and irregular bleeding, the temperature shift is very helpful in showing if and when ovulation has occurred.

On the debit side, it has to be recognised that when used alone as a single index of fertility in the single-index approach, the temperature method restricts considerably the time available for sexual intercourse if an unplanned pregnancy is to be avoided. The temperature gives no indication of infertility until *after* the temperature shift. Consequently, abstinence from sexual intercourse must continue for about two-thirds of the cycle. Also, as the temperature method does not detect the beginning of the fertile phase, it is not a very successful method for helping to achieve a pregnancy.

The fact that the temperature method does not indicate the beginning of the fertile phase makes it unsuitable in situations where ovulation might be delayed or erratic (for example, after childbirth, or stopping the pill), since it necessitates long periods of abstinence during the first infertile phase which the temperature chart fails to detect.

How safe is the temperature method?

The temperature method alone can only detect the end of the fertile phase and the beginning of the absolutely infertile phase after ovulation. If sexual intercourse is restricted to this latter part of the cycle, the temperature method can be up to 99 per cent effective in avoiding an unwanted pregnancy. This compares favourably with sterilisation (99.7 per cent effective) and the contraceptive pill (94–99 per cent effective, depending on the type of pill being taken).

If combined with the calendar method for detecting the beginning of the fertile phase, its effectiveness drops to 93 per cent. This is caused partly by difficulties in interpreting temperature readings if they are irregular or confused by disturbances, and partly by failure to observe abstinence in the first part of the cycle. Nevertheless, this level of effectiveness for a method that has no concomitant medical hazards for the user is most acceptable and compares well with barrier methods of contraception, low-dose contraceptive pills and IUDs.

The effectiveness of the temperature method when used in combination with other indicators is discussed in the chapters on multiple-index methods.

As a means of optimising the chances of achieving a pregnancy the temperature method is of little practical value, because it can only detect ovulation retrospectively. Many infertility clinics still suggest that a couple experiencing problems with conception keep a temperature chart and time sexual contact according to information it supplies. This, however, generally produces very poor results and increases the couple's frustration and despair.

5

The cervical mucus method

The cervical mucus method of natural family planning relies on the woman observing the changes in her cervical mucus throughout the menstrual cycle, and using these changes as indicators of the fertile and infertile phases. Most women are aware to some degree of variations in vaginal discharge at different times in their cycles. These variations reflect the different types of mucus being produced in the cervix as a result of the changing levels of oestrogen and progesterone in the bloodstream. Once taught how to recognise the different types of mucus and their significance – advice from a trained adviser is important here – many women find it is a most acceptable and effective way of assessing their fertility.

This method is also known as the ovulation method or the Billings method, after the two doctors who pioneered the use of mucus in the assessment of fertility. The method described here is based on that set out in the Family Fertility Education Learning Package and differs slightly from the Billings method, although it is similar in most respects. Any woman interested in using this method should seek advice from trained advisers, and a list of organisations that will provide information and assistance is included at the end of the book. Most women quickly learn the pattern of their own mucus cycles, but specially trained teachers can help in the effective application of the method as a means of planning a family.

The purpose of cervical mucus

The mucus produced by the glands in a woman's cervix plays a remarkable and vital role in the reproductive process. Its most important function is to control the transport of the sperm from the vagina, where they are deposited, to the fallopian tubes so that fertilisation of the ovum can be accomplished. Two types of mucus are produced at different times in the cycle: one is favourable to the sperm, the other is hostile. Before and during ovulation the mucus produced is thin, stretchy and watery and contains channels that guide the sperm towards their goal, the waiting ovum. After ovulation has taken place, the type of mucus changes dramatically. It becomes thick and sticky, inhibiting the movement of the sperm and literally barring the way through the cervix. In this way, the cervix acts as a biological valve, at certain times in the cycle encouraging the passage of the sperm and at other times blocking their path.

Without the presence of the favourable type of mucus the sperm can only survive in the vagina for a few hours. The sperm need the mucus to help them move and to provide them with nourishment to replenish their energy supplies for the rest of their journey. The mucus also gives them protection. Strangely, the vagina offers the sperm the most hostile of environments. The vagina's natural acidity would kill the sperm within a few hours if it were not for the neutralising quality of the mucus. The cervical mucus has a further vital role of quality control. Every time a man ejaculates, his semen contains some damaged sperm. The mucus acts as a very effective filtering mechanism, sifting out the damaged sperm so that only the healthy ones have a chance of fertilising the ovum.

For women wishing to use the mucus method as a way of planning their families the important point is that the cervix produces two distinct types of mucus – fertile-type mucus and infertile-type mucus – at different times in the cycle.

The mucus pattern

Using our understanding of the fertility cycle, a pattern of mucus production can be established which corresponds to the phases in the cycle.

Phase before ovulation (Preovulatory phase)
Just after menstruation the levels of oestrogen and pro-gesterone in the bloodstream are very low, so little, if any, mucus is produced. This time is characterised by a positive sensation of dryness at the vulva, indicating the absence of mucus. For some women, however, a thick, tacky, opaque mucus may be present in the very early stages of this phase. When held between thumb and forefinger and stretched this infertile-type mucus breaks quickly (see Plate 1). When this type of mucus is present, the woman will be aware of a feeling of stickiness at the entrance to her vagina.

Fertile phase
As the follicles in the ovary start to ripen, they secrete increasing amounts of oestrogen, which triggers the cer-vical crypts in the cervix to step up mucus production (see Plate 2). This is the start of the fertile phase. The mucus now being produced nourishes the sperm, and if the couple have sexual intercourse at this time the sperm may be kept alive long enough to fertilise the ripe ovum. Therefore, as soon as *any* change can be observed in either the basic infertile pattern of dryness or the basic infertile pattern of mucus (i.e. sensation of stickiness changing to one of moistness), the woman must assume that she is now potentially fertile.

As the oestrogen levels continue to rise with the approach of ovulation, both the quality and quantity of the mucus change noticeably. The mucus is now more abundant and becomes increasingly thinner, stretchier, clearer and more watery (by the time of ovulation the mucus will be 98 per cent water) (see Plate 3). It is often discharged in threads and has an elastic quality; if held between thumb and fore-finger, it can be stretched for several centimetres before the strand breaks. Some women have likened this type of mucus to raw egg-white.

Usually colourless, the mucus can also be cloudy or pinkish, reddish, yellowish or brown if it contains any blood from mid-cycle spotting. The woman will notice a definite sensation of wetness and slipperiness at her vulva at this time. Any feeling of moistness indicates the onset of the fertile phase, so unprotected intercourse should be avoided if conception is not desired.

The height of fertility occurs on the last day of the fertile-type mucus and is known as the *peak mucus day*. However, the word 'peak' can be misleading: the peak mucus day may not be the day on which the greatest quantity of mucus can be detected; rather, it is the last day on which mucus displaying the characteristics of fertile-type mucus can be observed, i.e. the last day on which the mucus appears wet, slippery, clear and stretchy (see Plate 4). The peak mucus day corresponds closely with the peak secretion of oestrogen in the bloodstream. This oestrogen peak occurs approximately one day before the LH peak which, in turn, precedes ovulation by not more than 48 hours. Therefore, the peak mucus day precedes ovulation by not more than three days. If 24 hours are allowed for the survival of the ovum, then the absolutely infertile phase (postovulatory phase) of the cycle should begin on the evening of the fourth day after the peak mucus day.

The peak mucus day can only be identified retrospectively: it is only possible to know that the last day of fertile-type mucus has occurred, if the mucus has changed its characteristics on the following day. However, there is an abrupt change from the fertile-type characteristics to an infertile-type mucus that makes this very easy to recognise.

The absolutely infertile phase (postovulatory phase)
After the release of the ripe ovum the sudden drop in oestrogen causes a rapid change in the amount and quality of the mucus. The quantity of mucus is much reduced, sometimes disappearing altogether, while it becomes

thick, sticky and opaque like the infertile-type mucus in the first stages of the cycle. When this infertile-type mucus, or a feeling of dryness, has persisted for three days after the peak mucus day, it is assumed that ovulation has occurred and the ovum has died. A couple can therefore be sure that conception cannot occur for the rest of that cycle.

How to identify the mucus

You can learn to identify the types of mucus from the external symptoms presented at your vulva in two ways:

1   By sensation – even a tiny amount of mucus can cause a marked change in the sensations experienced. This is particularly helpful for those who do not produce very much mucus.
2   By observing the appearance of the mucus.

Sensation   As your fertility cycle progresses you will be able to detect three distinct sensations at your vulva:
    (a)   a distinct feeling of dryness;
    (b)   a distinct feeling of wetness;
    (c)   a feeling of being neither dry nor wet, i.e. a feeling of moistness.

These subjective sensations are a most important alerting system to the fertile and infertile phases of the cycle.

A distinct feeling of *dryness* indicates *infertility*. When there is no mucus there is little oestrogen in the bloodstream, so the follicles will not be active in producing a ripe ovum. Without mucus the sperm lack nourishment and protection and so quickly die.

A distinct feeling of *wetness* indicates *fertility*, even if no mucus is visible at the vulva. In some women the mucus contains so much water that it runs away quickly, making observation difficult.

A feeling of *moistness* has to be viewed as indicating *potential fertility* if it occurs before ovulation in the cycle.

It is important to note that after sexual intercourse and sometimes during sexual excitement, you may not feel dry even though no mucus is present. While learning to detect the sensation and appearance of mucus, you may find it difficult to differentiate these feelings from those produced by mucus symptoms. Therefore, it is advisable to abstain from intercourse for the first complete cycle so that you can become truly familiar with your mucus pattern.

Observing the appearance of the mucus You can observe your mucus when it has flowed down from the cervix and presents itself at the vaginal opening. Collect the mucus by wiping your vulva with a tissue both before and after urinating. (If you don't do it beforehand, much of the mucus may be washed away and lost. If you wipe yourself afterwards as well, you will be able to collect the mucus that has been moved down the vagina by the process of urinating.)

Check the mucus on the tissue for colour, glossiness, fluidity, transparency and stretchiness. To test for the latter, open your hand and allow the tissue to unfold and note whether the mucus holds the stretch or breaks quickly. Some mucus will probably have been deposited on your underwear, in which case this can also be checked for fertile-type characteristics.

Those women who find it difficult to observe mucus at the vulva can gently insert one or two fingers into the vagina and collect mucus on their fingertips from the cervix itself for observation. Some women find this the most reliable way to check their mucus. Certainly, in the preovulatory phase if you want to have sexual intercourse in the morning, it is wise to check for mucus in the cervix in this way. A feeling of dryness after a night's rest may just mean that the mucus has not yet travelled down the vagina.

Recording the mucus cycle
Observe your mucus several times a day. This may sound a tiresome exercise but you will find that it quickly becomes second nature. Last thing at night record your observations

for the day on a mucus method chart designed for the purpose. If, during the day, you have observed both fertile and infertile types of mucus, the most fertile type must be recorded for that day.

If you are using the mucus method as a single-index method, record the following information on the special charts:

1 Days of menstruation and intermenstrual bleeding.
2 Dry days.
3 Infertile-type mucus days.
4 Fertile-type mucus days.
5 Peak mucus day.
6 Three days following the peak mucus day.
7 Days on which sexual intercourse or close genital contact occurred.
8 Day after sexual intercourse, when this occurs before the peak mucus day.

Several styles of chart are currently available which use a variety of different symbols for recording the pertinent events in the cycle. Some use coloured stamps or pencils, different symbols or simply letters, or a combination of these (see Chart 8). All are designed to ensure a quick, easy and accurate method of recording the information required to assess the phases of the cycle.

It is also advisable to reinforce the symbols with a written description of the mucus appearance. One or two words will suffice, such as 'moist and thick' or 'wet and stretchy'.

Chart 9 is a typical mucus method chart of the type used in the Family Fertility Education Learning Package (WHO/BLAT). It uses coloured pencils to record mucus characteristics.

Rules for using the mucus method of family planning
The mucus method can identify the relatively infertile phase, the fertile phase and the absolutely infertile phase of the cycle. For this reason it is extremely useful both

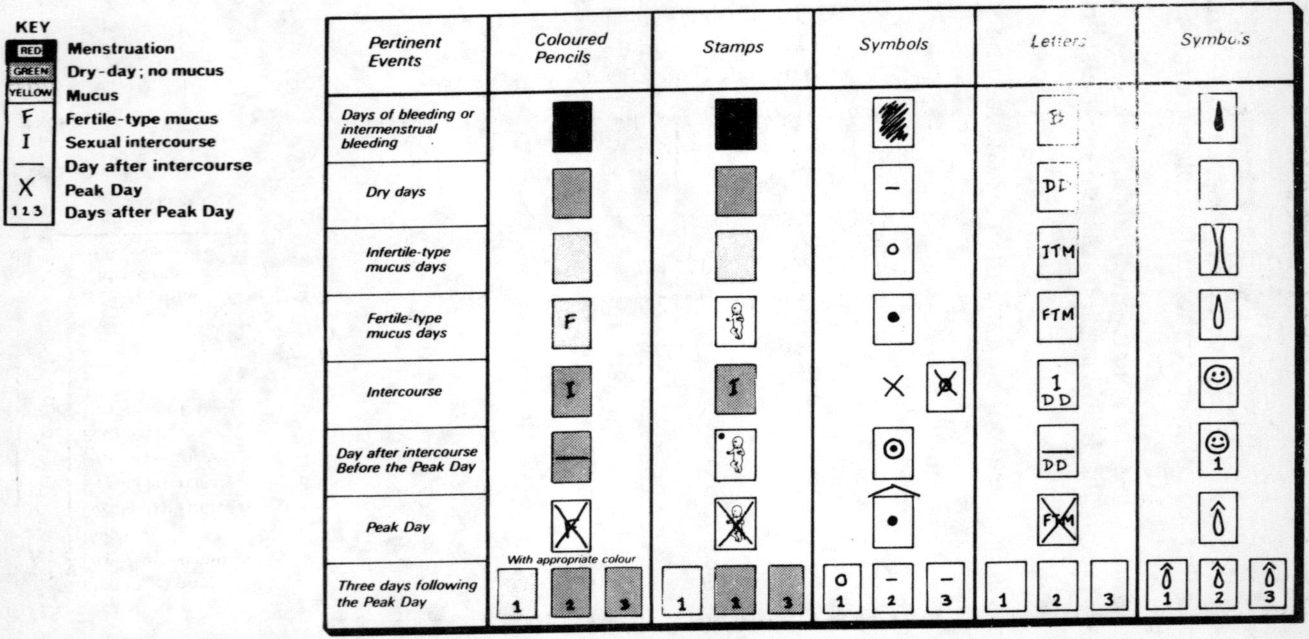

Pertinent Events	Coloured Pencils			Stamps			Symbols			Letters			Symbols		
Days of bleeding or intermenstrual bleeding	■			■			░			ℬ			↑		
Dry days							|			DD			☐		
Infertile-type mucus days	F						o			ITM			⋈		
Fertile-type mucus days	I			🐟			●			FTM			⬯		
Intercourse	|						×			$\frac{I}{DD}$			☺		
Day after intercourse Before the Peak Day	⊠			🐟			⊙			$\frac{}{DD}$			☺1		
Peak Day	With appropriate colour			⊠			◁●			⋈			⬯		
	1	2	3	1	2	3	0 1	1 2	1 3	1	2	3	⬯1	⬯2	⬯3

Chart 8 The variety of symbols that can be used for charting the cervical mucus symptom of fertility.

KEY

RED	Menstruation
GREEN	Dry-day; no mucus
YELLOW	Mucus
F	Fertile-type mucus
I	Sexual intercourse
/	Day after intercourse
X	Peak Day
1·2·3	Days after Peak Day

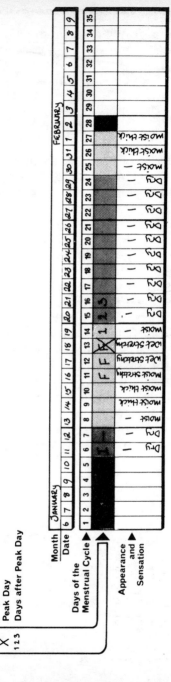

Chart 9 A typical mucus method chart.

for avoiding an unwanted pregnancy and as a means of achieving conception.

The use of the mucus method to avoid pregnancy The rules outlined below are based on those used by the FFELP, which differ slightly from those proposed by the Billings. Any variation is indicated.

1 *During the learning phase*, abstinence from sexual inter-course and genital contact is helpful for the first cycle or month of charting mucus symptoms, because seminal fluid and other secretions related to sexual stimulation may make it difficult to establish the presence of mucus.

2 *The first fertile day* in the cycle is the first day on which either the sensation or appearance of mucus occurs. It is important to note that any sensation of wetness, even if no mucus is visible, must be taken as indicating potential fertility. (This differs from the rules of the Billings method which considers *all* days of menstruation to be fertile days.) According to the FFELP the first five days of a true menstrual bleed (recognised by the presence of a peak mucus day followed by a postovulatory phase of ten days in the previous cycle) are infertile days unless mucus is observed during these days.

3 After menstruation, *alternate dry days before the peak mucus day are considered to be infertile*. Intercourse is only recommended on the evening of these alternate dry days. The day following sexual intercourse is considered to be fertile because of the difficulty of identifying mucus on that day.

4 *The time from the evening of the fourth day after the peak mucus symptom* until the end of the cycle is considered to be infertile. Should the sperm be capable of surviving in the infertile-type mucus present at this stage of the cycle, there is no living ovum to be ferti-lised.

The use of the mucus method to achieve pregnancy The mucus method is the most efficient method for helping to achieve conception because it indicates the preovulatory phase. To maximise the chances of conception, the couple should have sexual intercourse on, or as close as possible to, the peak mucus day, when the woman is at the height of her fertility and the fertile-type mucus is at a peak. It is also believed to be advantageous to restrict sexual intercourse to the days of this highly fertile mucus. This is particularly true for seemingly infertile couples, where subfertility in both partners may be the problem. (Infertility and its possible causes and treatment are discussed in Chapter 8.)

Possible variations in the mucus cycle
As with all indicators of fertility, not all women show typical or consistent mucus patterns. Some women, for example, never have any dry days; they are always aware of a sensation of moistness or wetness at the vulva, indicating the continuous presence of mucus. Such a pattern is described as the basic *infertile pattern of mucus* (in contrast to the basic infertile pattern of dryness) and is shown in Chart 10. Women with such a mucus pattern may need longer to learn their own patterns and be confident in differentiating between fertile and infertile types of mucus in the preovulatory phase.

In rare cases a woman has no mucus discharge. This usually occurs only in women who are subfertile or infertile, and the lack of mucus may indicate a deficiency in their hormonal system.

The advantages and disadvantages of the mucus method
It does take time – on average about three cycles – for a woman to become familiar with her own mucus pattern and to feel at ease with the method. Some women will need less time, others longer before they are confident of their observations. This obviously requires a degree of commitment to the method from *both* partners, particularly where periods of sexual abstinence are needed. However,

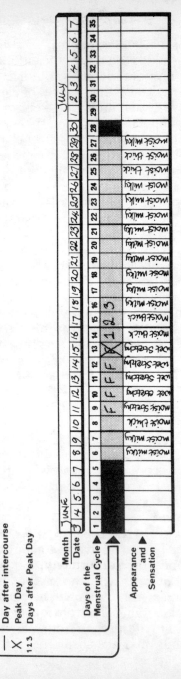

KEY

RED	Menstruation
GREEN	Dry-day; no mucus
YELLOW	Mucus
F	Fertile-type mucus
I	Sexual intercourse
X	Day after intercourse
X	Peak Day
1 2 3	Days after Peak Day

Chart 10 The basic infertile pattern of mucus.

the teamwork required can be one of the bonuses of the method, and many couples have given testimony to how co-operating together to make the method work creates a sense of mutual understanding and closeness.

To be sure of using the method effectively, it is necessary to seek advice from trained teachers. Once trained, however, it is a very simple method that does not require any special tools or devices. Charts and recording techniques can easily be improvised to suit individual requirements.

The necessity of checking the mucus appearance several times each day may seem a chore, but in general most women quickly learn to observe their mucus automatically every time they go to the toilet. Many say what pleasure they get from being in touch with the natural cycles of their fertility and understanding how their bodies work.

It has been known for pregnancies to result from intercourse on the last of the dry days in the cycle. This is probably because sufficient fertile-type mucus is present in the cervix itself to prolong the lifespan of the sperm, even though no mucus is visible at the vulva. When using the mucus method as a single-index method, it is therefore advisable for the woman to check her cervix in the preovulatory days to see whether the cervix is dry (in which case it is a truly dry, and therefore infertile, day). If there is mucus on the cervix, the day should be considered fertile whether or not mucus is present at the vulva.

As with the BBT pattern, the mucus pattern can be disturbed by a variety of factors, though stress is perhaps the most common one. This can give rise to the *double peak cycle* (see Chart 11), in which ovulation is delayed by a lack of hormonal input. Fertility appears to begin, as indicated by the appearance of fertile-type mucus, then stops only to start again later. In cases such as this it is useful to fall back on one of the other indicators of fertility to determine when ovulation has occurred.

Vaginal discharges as a result of infection, such as monilial infection (thrush), may cloud the changes in

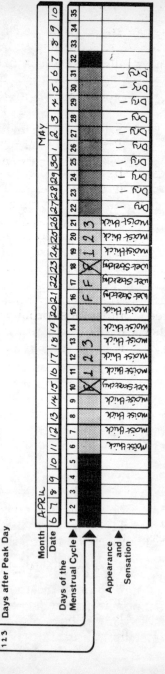

Chart 11   The double-peak of mucus.

the mucus pattern. This is usually only a problem for women who are just learning to use the mucus method. Those women already familiar with their own patterns can usually distinguish between natural changes resulting from the mucus cycle and those caused by an infection.

Finally, some drugs can disrupt the mucus cycle. Drugs used for colds and sinusitis to dry up the mucous membranes in the nose may have the same effect on the mucous membranes of the cervix. Also, some cortisone preparations can inhibit mucus production. However, insulin does not appear to affect the mucus cycle in any way and many diabetics can use NFP methods most successfully.

Most normally fertile women can learn to identify their own mucus patterns quickly and easily. In the World Health Organisation's study of users of the Billings method, 97 per cent of the participants were able to observe and interpret their cervical mucus patterns at the end of three months. Most problems of identification and interpretation can be overcome with the help of a trained counsellor, a little practice and confidence.

How safe is the mucus method?
Unlike the temperature method, the mucus method can be used to identify both beginning and end of the fertile phase in the cycle. Thus, couples using the method have the possibility of sexual intercourse in both preovulatory and postovulatory infertile phases.

A study conducted in 1976 among women using the mucus method in Australia showed that, under ideal conditions (when the method had been well-taught and the couple observed the rules correctly and precisely) the effectiveness of the mucus method was in the region of 97 per cent.

However, surveys by the World Health Organisation show that in practice this figure drops to around 88 per cent, either because of misinterpretation of the mucus symptom, or a lack of motivation in practising abstinence during the potentially fertile days in the cycle.

Nevertheless, for many couples the fact that the mucus method is simple to apply and has no medical complications more than compensates for an effectiveness somewhat less than the contraceptive pill or IUD. (The possibility of improving the efficiency of the mucus method by combining it with other indicators of fertility is discussed in Chapter 6.)

For those couples wishing to achieve a pregnancy the mucus method is by far the best, as it can predict the peak of fertility in the cycle.

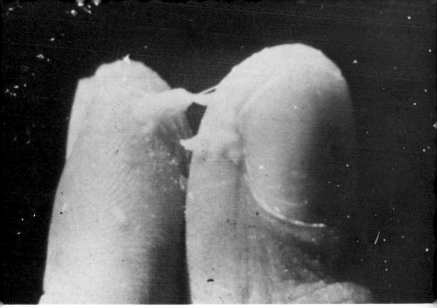

An example of mucus during the early part of the pre-ovulatory phase. With this
e of mucus there is usually a sensation of dryness at the vulva. If a specimen can
obtained for examination, it will show all the characteristics of infertile-type
cus: thick, tacky and opaque, breaking on any attempt to stretch between thumb
forefinger. Mucus obtained during the post-ovulatory phase will demonstrate
same infertile-type characteristics.

Here the mucus is exhibiting some fertile-type characteristics: it has become
nner and can be stretched for a couple of centimetres without breaking,
icating increasing fertility.

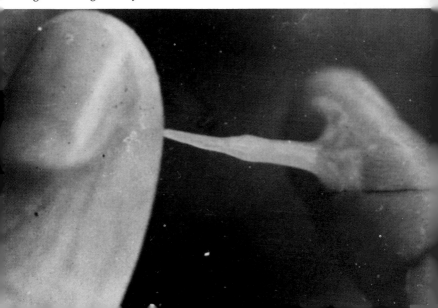

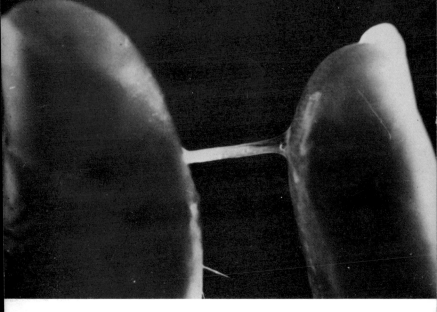

3 Here the mucus is not only stretchy but is also beginning to become m[ore] transparent (increased water content), predicting approaching ovulation.

4 This photograph shows a clear, transparent, stretchy and glistening muc[us] When present, there is a distinct sensation of lubrication and wetness at the vu[lva] indicating very high fertility and imminent ovulation.

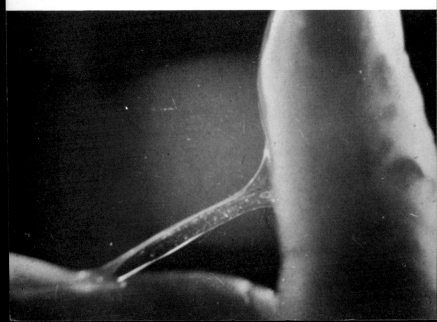

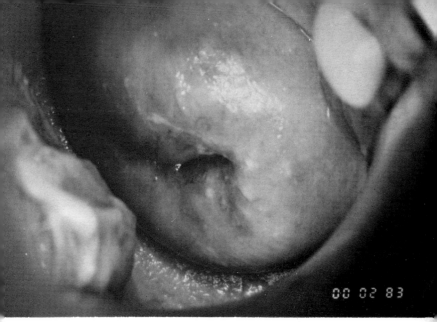

00 02 83

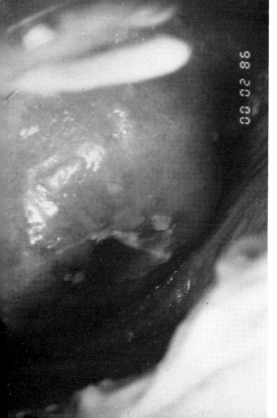

00 02 86

Plates 5–8 are sequential photographs of the cyclical changes in the cervix of a woman who is in her thirties, and the mother of three children. Her normal cycle length is between 24 and 27 days and she practises natural family planning.

5 (above) This is day 12 of her cycle. The opening of the os and the presence of a small amount of glistening mucus suggest that ovulation is probably near.

6 (left) This is the morning of day 13 showing an open os with stretchy, but not completely clear, mucus.

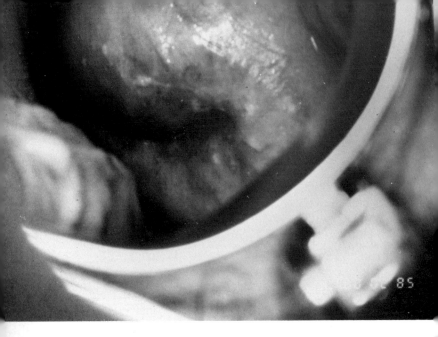

7 Because she experienced mid-cycle pain she thought she had ovulated. Th[is] photograph, taken in the late evening of day 13, indicates that this was probably [the] case as the cervix has closed a little, although not yet completely.

8 On day 14 the os is closed and dry. As she has had three children her cer[vix] never becomes completely closed.

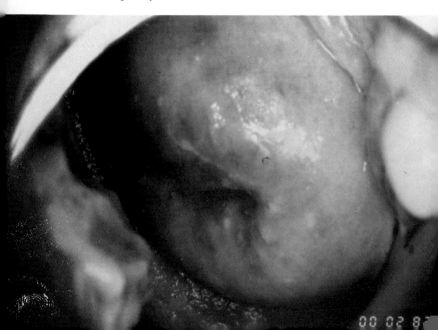

6

Multiple-index methods

In contrast to the single-index methods discussed so far, multiple-index methods combine two or more indicators of fertility, thus increasing the accuracy with which a woman can determine the different phases of her cycle. The choice of indicators depends on which signs and symptoms are predominant in each individual woman and the ease with which she can observe them.

From our experience of teaching and researching into natural family planning methods, the double-check method is the most effective multiple-index method. The rules for this method are discussed in full later in this chapter, though all the various multiple-index methods are also outlined.

Several indicators of fertility which can be used in the multiple-index approach will be described first, then the various combinations of indicators that can be employed for the purposes of family planning will be examined.

Cyclical changes in the cervix

As with cervical mucus, the different levels of oestrogen and progesterone in the bloodstream during the fertility cycle produce detectable changes in the cervix.

How to examine your cervix
First, empty your bladder. A full bladder makes the cervix

difficult to reach. Either you or your partner can observe the changes in the cervix, though it is important that the same person makes the observations over a complete cycle to ensure that the changes are genuine physiological ones and not just due to the individual's perception.

Several positions can be used to make the examination easier. Try them all and then decide which is the most convenient and comfortable for you:

- Standing, with your left foot on a chair.
- Squatting down (as when sitting on the toilet).
- Lying on your back with your knees up and your legs apart.

Whichever method you choose, be sure to stick to that position for the entire cycle. Examine your cervix every day, preferably at the same time.

Wash your hands and then gently insert the index and middle fingers into your vagina (if you find it difficult to use two fingers, just use the middle finger), and reach up towards the top of the vagina. The cervix will feel like the tip of a nose or a small chin with a dimple. The dimple is the cervical os, the small hole in the centre of the cervix. The consistency of the cervix changes during the cycle, but it never feels as soft as the vaginal walls. Also the walls of the vagina are ridged, making them feel completely different to the smooth texture of the cervix.

What are you looking for?
By examining your cervix every day you will be able to detect changes in:

- The position of the cervix.
- The texture of the cervix.
- The width of the cervical os.

Start your observations at the beginning of a cycle, as the cervix is easier to reach at this time. When the oestrogen and progesterone levels are at a minimum during the early infertile days of the cycle, the cervix is low in the pelvic cavity, close to the vaginal opening and in easy reach of your fingers. At this time it will feel firm to the touch and you will be able to feel that the cervical os is closed.

Under the influence of the increasing quantities of oestrogen secreted by the ripening follicle in the ovary, the cervix will move noticeably upwards away from the vaginal opening, sometimes completely out of reach of your fingers. It will reach its highest point at the time of the oestrogen peak, around the time of the peak mucus symptom, i.e. at the height of your fertility. This dramatic upward movement is probably the easiest of the cervical changes to detect.

In this fertile phase of the cycle, the cervix will feel progressively softer, becoming spongy and rubbery around the time of ovulation. You will also be able to detect the gradual opening of the cervical os, which is at its maximum width at ovulation.

Immediately after ovulation and as a consequence of the rising quantities of progesterone in the bloodstream, the cervix abruptly returns to the position and texture of the preovulatory infertile phase. You will feel that the cervix has become firm again and is now in its low position in the pelvic cavity, once more within easy reach of your fingers. The cervical os also closes at this time. (If you have had children, your cervical os may never close completely, though you will still be able to detect a definite opening and closing of the os during the cycle, so this will not be a problem.)

These changes in the cervical os can be seen in Plates 5–8.

Use of changes in the cervix in natural family planning
As an indicator of fertility, the changes in the cervix are best used in combination with other indicators, such as mucus or temperature. Some women, when completely familiar with their own patterns and confident in observing changes in their cervices, do use it as a single-index method, though we do not recommend

it. It is, however, a particularly useful indicator of fertility for nursing mothers and women approaching the menopause, when other indicators may have been disrupted by the hormonal changes occurring in the body. (This is discussed more fully in Chapter 7.)

By observing the changes in the cervix over a complete cycle, it is possible to detect the beginning and end of the fertile phase. *Any* change in the cervix from its original infertile state indicates the onset of fertility, so couples wishing to avoid a pregnancy should abstain from unprotected intercourse from this time. The first changes in the cervix commonly occur four or five days before ovulation.

The rapid return of the cervix to its infertile state after ovulation is a good reference point for detecting the end of the fertile phase. From the moment these changes can be detected, four days should be allowed before a couple can assume that the absolutely infertile phase has begun and they can resume sexual relations without fear of an unwanted pregnancy.

In summary, fertility is indicated by:

1 Raising of the cervix in the pelvic cavity, away from the vaginal opening.
2 Softening in the texture of the cervix.
3 Opening of the cervical os.

Infertility is indicated by:

1 Lowering of the cervix towards the vaginal opening.
2 Firming up in the texture of the cervix.
3 Closing of the cervical os.

How to record changes in the cervix
Chart 12 shows how changes in the cervix can be recorded during a cycle. The position of the cervix (shown by dots for low or high positions), its consistency (described as either 'firm' or 'soft') and the size of the cervical os (drawn as a dot or small circle) are all charted for every day of

74

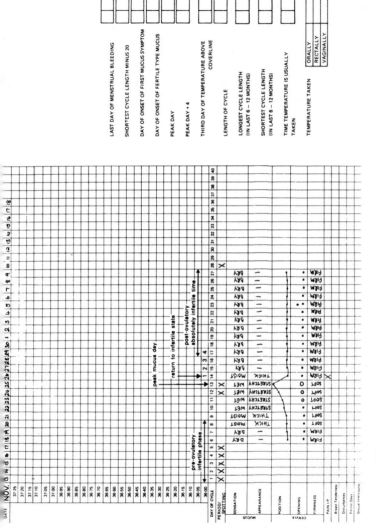

Chart 12   Showing changes in the cervix as one of the indicators of fertility.

the cycle. These observations give a clear picture of the different phases of the cycle.

In Chart 12 the first changes are observed on day 8; day 13 is the peak mucus day and also the day on which the cervix is showing the maximum characteristics of fertility. Observations on day 14 indicate a return to the infertile state: the cervix has become firm again, is in its low position and the cervical os has closed. Allowing four days, the couple can be sure that the woman is in her absolutely infertile phase from day 18.

How effective are cervical changes as an indicator of fertility?

Although individual women use cyclical changes in the cervix most successfully to detect the fertile phase of their cycles, the method has only recently begun to be taught as part of natural family planning in the clinics. Indeed, some clinics still do not include it in their teaching. Consequently, there is, as yet, no statistical analysis of the effectiveness of this indicator as a single-index method of family planning.

Used in combination with the mucus method, cervical changes can help to overcome some of the problems that undermine the effectiveness of the mucus method, such as dry days and double peak charts. Again, we shall have to wait for a decade or so before we can assess the efficiency of this combination.

However, it is true to say that for some women, especially those whose sexual partners are willing to take an active role in the daily observations, cervical changes appear to be a more objective method of assessing the fertile time than mucus observations. Certainly, a joint approach and a shared responsibility for family planning greatly increase the motivation of the couple, which in turn improves the effectiveness of the method they are using.

In situations where a delay in ovulation is possible, such as after childbirth or during the menopause, changes in the cervix can provide the vital indicator for distinguishing between returning fertility and actual ovulation in a preovulatory phase that may last for several weeks.

Calendar calculations

Calendar calculations are the basis of the old-fashioned rhythm method, from which natural family planning methods in general have gained such a poor reputation. The fact that the rhythm method is both unreliable and unacceptably restrictive is now recognised, and calendar calculations are no longer recommended as a single-index method. However, this is not to deny that calendar calculations can provide useful back-up information when used as one of the indicators in a multiple-index approach.

The calendar calculations are based on the following information:

1 The fact that ovulation occurs 10–16 days before the next menstruation.
2 The probability of when ovulation will occur in the present cycle based on observations of the cycle lengths over the previous 6–12 cycles.
3 The lifespan of the sperm under favourable mucus conditions and the lifespan of the ovum.

These data allow formulae to be devised for determining the fertile days of the cycle.

To determine the first day of the fertile time in preovulatory phase: take the shortest cycle length recorded over not less than six previous cycles and subtract from this the number 20. (The figure 20 is reached by assuming that the period from ovulation to menstruation will not generally be longer than 16 days and adding to this four days for the lifespan of the sperm.)

If, for example, you have recorded cycles of 26–30 days over the previous six months, the first day of the fertile phase will be 26 minus 20, which is day 6 of the cycle. Therefore, in the first part of this cycle, the safe days would be days 1–5, day 1 being the first day of your menstrual bleeding.

If you have recorded your cycles for 12 months previously, you can take the shortest cycle recorded minus 19 as the first day of the fertile phase.

To determine the end of the fertile phase: take the longest cycle length recorded over the previous six cycles and subtract 10. (The figure 10 is derived from the assumption that the shortest time from ovulation to the next menstruation is 10 days.)

Therefore, if 30 days was the longest cycle observed in the preceding six cycles, the last day of the fertile phase will be 30 minus 10, which is day 20. Thus, the safe days in the postovulatory phase of the cycle will be from day 21 to the end of that cycle.

Calendar calculations and modern natural family planning methods

Calendar calculations are *not* recommended as a single-index method of natural family planning. Nor is this method now used to detect the end of the fertile time in a multiple-index approach, as both the temperature shift and the peak mucus symptom are much more reliable indicators and equally simple to use.

This said, calendar calculations can be an effective method for predicting the beginning of the fertile phase, especially when combined with other indicators of fertility.

Minor indicators of fertility

When discussing how our bodies work in Chapter 2, mention was made of the minor physiological and psychological changes which provide further signals of events taking place in the woman's body in relation to her menstrual cycle. Not all women experience these minor symptoms, but for those who do they can become valuable supporting indicators of fertility, confirming the information provided by their other observations.

Ovulation pain

This is by no means a universal symptom, but it is particularly useful for those women who do experience it. Such pain may be sharp and last for a few hours, or mild and cramp-like for a day or two. It can be felt at the level of the ovaries on either the left or right side of the body, depending on which ovary has released the ripe ovum for that cycle. Both the symptothermal chart and the multiple-index method chart allow room for noting the occurrence of ovulation pain (see Chart 12).

Mid-cycle spotting or bleeding

Again, this is not a symptom experienced by all women. Where it does occur it is closely related to the peak mucus symptom and ovulation. Physiologically, it is caused by the sudden sharp drop in oestrogen levels around the time of ovulation and so indicates peak fertility.

This can also be recorded on the various charts (see Chart 12).

Breast tenderness

This is a fairly common symptom of the fertility cycle. It can be caused by high levels of oestrogen, or high levels of progesterone. However, depending on which hormone is causing the tenderness, both the timing and the type of discomfort vary. Breast tenderness as a consequence of high oestrogen levels can be observed in the middle of the cycle and so indicates the presence of the fertile phase. This type of tenderness is characterised by a painful, tingling sensation.

Breast symptoms observed in the last part of the cycle are caused by high levels of progesterone and are often described as feelings of fullness and heaviness rather than actual pain. These are obviously occurring in the infertile phase.

Breast tenderness can also be included on the various charts as a useful confirmatory symptom for the major indicators (see Chart 13).

Psychological and mood changes

At some time most women experience emotional and mood changes related to high concentrations of either oestrogen or progesterone. Those who are affected by the high oestrogen level in the middle of the cycle often report an increase in their libido and a craving for affection and love. Given that this occurs in the fertile phase of the cycle, it is important for women affected in this way to discuss their problem with their partners so that they can work out ways of expressing their love for each other without the need for sexual intercourse.

The majority of women experience an increased desire for love in the premenstrual phase. Others become depressed, tired or irritable, while some experience sleeplessness and increased appetite. There are as many manifestations as there are women. The important point is that these feelings can be very powerful, even undermining the woman's general sense of well-being. But once she is aware of their physiological basis and can fit them into the pattern of her fertility cycle, she may well find that she can come to terms with any change and determine her own response rather than feeling a victim of her mood swings.

Multiple-index methods

Many combinations of indicators of fertility can be used, giving rise to several varieties of multiple-index methods of natural family planning.

Multiple-index methods

Symptothermal methods
Although the temperature method is highly effective, few couples now use it as a single-index method because the problem of detecting the beginning of the fertile phase demands lengthy periods of abstinence from sexual activity in the first phase of the cycle. As a result the temperature method is supplemented by one or more indicators of impending ovulation, such as mucus discharge, changes in the cervix, and/or calendar calculations.

The *calculothermal method* involves the use of calendar calculations to predict the beginning of the fertile phase and the temperature shift to identify its end.

The *mucothermal method* uses the mucus symptom to detect the beginning of the fertile phase and the temperature shift to determine its end.

Other combinations include using the calendar calculations and the mucus symptom and/or the changes in the cervix. Minor indicators may also be added if these are present. However, as the title of the method implies, changes in the basal body temperature are the key to the method and must always be used.

Mucus method plus calendar calculations
The mucus method can be combined with calendar calculations. The latter are used to predict the beginning of the fertile phase while the peak mucus symptom indicates the end of the fertile phase and the beginning of the absolutely infertile phase.

Mucus method plus cervical changes
Women whose lifestyle (shift-workers, women doing night duty, air hostesses, for example) makes the temperature method difficult, and who are reluctant to use the mucus symptom as a single indicator, can combine changes in the cervix with the mucus method to detect both the beginning and end of the fertile phase. To these can be added any of the minor indicators of fertility that are experienced.

The double-check method
This is recommended as the most effective method of natural family planning, for the following reasons:

- It can be tailored to suit each individual woman and her own unique fertility pattern. It allows her to become familiar with all her indicators of fertility and to select those she finds most suitable and convenient.
- It offers the best possibility of efficiency and accuracy, thus providing much greater security and freedom for those using it. At least two (and possibly more) indicators are used to determine both the beginning and the end of the fertile phase. This double checking of indicators ensures the greatest possible accuracy and helps to over-ride the margin of human error inherent in the interpretation of all indicators of fertility.

In the double-check method outlined the following indicators of fertility are observed.

To detect the beginning of the fertile phase:
1 Calendar calculations – the shortest cycle minus 19, where at least six cycle lengths have been recorded and the woman has noted a temperature shift and a high temperature phase in her previous cycle to indicate that ovulation occurred in that cycle; *and*
2 The first *mucus symptom*, whether detected by sensation or appearance.
  Whichever of these indicators (1) or (2) comes *first* marks the beginning of the fertile phase.
3 Changes in the cervix can be used to check the other indicators, but this is not essential.

To detect the end of the fertile phase and the beginning of the postovulatory infertile phase:
1 The *temperature shift* – the infertile phase begins on the morning of the third consecutive high temperature after the temperature shift; *and*
2 The *peak mucus symptom* – the infertile phase begins

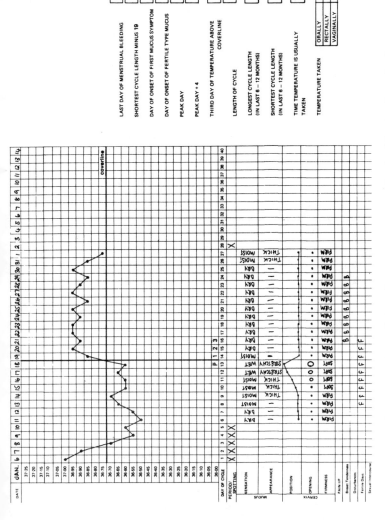

Chart 13 A typical chart for a woman using the double-check method.

on the evening of the fourth day after the peak mucus symptom.

Whichever of these indicators (1) or (2) comes *last* marks the beginning of the infertile phase.

3   Again, changes in the cervix can be used to confirm the information supplied by the other indicators, if desired.

Charting for the double-check method   Chart 13 has been completed by a woman using the double-check method of natural family planning. The information on her chart enables her to determine the beginning of the fertile phase from:

1   The calendar calculations shown on the right of the chart. Her shortest cycle length recorded over the previous 12 cycles is 27; 27 minus 19 = 8, and therefore day 8 is the first fertile day in the preovulatory phase.
2   The mucus symptom. This is the sensation of moistness for the first time on day 8, confirming the calendar calculations.

Therefore, this woman and her partner know that she is in the fertile phase of her cycle from day 8 and that if pregnancy is to be avoided, they should abstain from unprotected intercourse until the end of that phase is indicated.

The end of the fertile phase and the beginning of the postovulatory infertile phase are determined by:

1   The temperature shift, which in Chart 13 occurs on day 13. Three consecutive days of high phase temperatures takes her to the end of her fertile phase, so the postovulatory infertile phase apparently begins on the morning of day 16.
2   The mucus symptom calculations give a slightly different picture, however. The peak mucus day also occurs

on day 13, confirming the temperature shift. Following the rules for the mucus method, the evening of the fourth day after the peak mucus symptom marks the start of the infertile phase after ovulation. As the *last* indicator marks the end of the fertile phase in the double-check method, the infertile phase in Chart 13 starts on the evening of day 17 and lasts until the end of that cycle.

So, the woman keeping this particular chart can be assured that unprotected sexual intercourse after the evening of day 17 of her cycle will not result in a pregnancy.

The double-check method is of particular value to women who have atypical charts which pose problems of interpretation. As more than one indicator is used to determine each of the phases in the cycle, a more flexible approach to interpretation can be adopted and some modification made to the rules that have to be applied if only a single indicator is used.

When used alone, a temperature shift is identified by an increase in BBT of at least 0.2°C (0.35°F) over the last low phase temperature, and this temperature increase has to be maintained for three consecutive readings. If this rule was applied to the temperature readings in Chart 14, it would be very difficult to be certain that a true temperature shift had occurred. However, this woman is using the double-check method, with calendar calculations and the mucus symptom as back-up indicators, so she can take a slightly different approach. Providing an upward shift in BBT of at least 0.1°C(0.2°F) is recorded, the coverline can be placed over all the low temperatures (excluding the first four and any disturbances). If this shows that at least *one* of the three higher temperatures is 0.2°C (0.35°F) above the last low temperature and all three higher readings are above the coverline, it can be interpreted as a true temperature shift.

When the double-check method is applied to the readings in Chart 14, the beginning of the fertile phase is determined as day 8 by (1) calendar calculations and

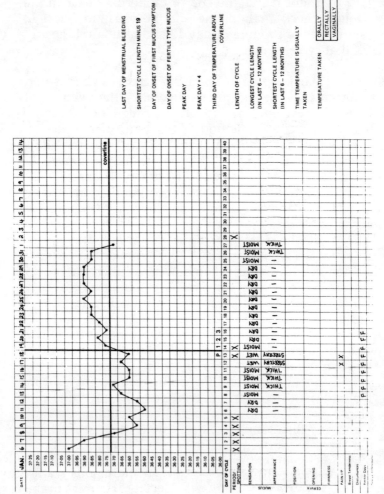

LAST DAY OF MENSTRUAL BLEEDING	0	5	
SHORTEST CYCLE LENGTH MINUS 19	0	8	
DAY OF ONSET OF FIRST MUCUS SYMPTOM	0	8	
DAY OF ONSET OF FERTILE TYPE MUCUS	1	2	
PEAK DAY	1	3	
PEAK DAY + 4	1	7	
THIRD DAY OF TEMPERATURE ABOVE COVERLINE	1	6	
LENGTH OF CYCLE	2	7	
LONGEST CYCLE LENGTH (IN LAST 6 – 12 MONTHS)	3	1	
SHORTEST CYCLE LENGTH (IN LAST 6 – 12 MONTHS)	2	7	
TIME TEMPERATURE IS USUALLY TAKEN	6	00	

TEMPERATURE TAKEN	ORALLY	✓
	RECTALLY	
	VAGINALLY	

Chart 14 Use of the double-check method to overcome difficulties in interpreting charts.

(2) the mucus symptom. The beginning of the infertile, postovulatory phase is identified as day 16 by the temperature method. As there is a temperature shift between days 13 and 14 of 0.15°C (0.25°F), the coverline can be placed over the low temperatures, between 36.7°C (98.1°F) and 36.75°C (98.2°F) on the chart. Thus, a low temperature phase can be identified, the last day of which is day 13. The temperature on day 15 is 0.2°C (0.35°F) above that on day 13 and the temperature readings on days 14, 15 and 16 remain above the coverline. Confirmation that this is a true temperature shift is provided by the mucus observations, which show that the peak mucus symptom occurs on day 13. Following the rules for the mucus symptom, the infertile phase begins on the evening of day 17. As this is the last indicator observed, it is regarded as marking the beginning of the infertile phase.

So, this woman can be assured that there is no risk of pregnancy resulting from sexual relations after the evening of day 17.

How efficient are the multiple-index methods?
Obviously, several different combinations of the indicators of fertility can be used; the 'double-check method', described on Pages 82–87, is the most efficient combination. The success rate is 99.3% to 99.5% when the method is correctly taught and consistently used. Even allowing for user failure recent surveys have shown that couples can achieve a success rate of 98.3% which is as good as the combined oral contraceptive pill and better than the minipill and the coil. At present a multicentre study by all European countries is being carried out to confirm the efficiency rate of the 'double-check method' which is now used by most European countries.

Modifications of the double-check method for unusual cycles
When a woman's cycles are exceptionally long and/or irregular, the use of the double-check method (first appearance of mucus or shortest cycle minus 19 – see p. 82 ff) very often entails several days of abstinence which, in

retrospect, can be seen to have been unnecessary. Two substitutions for the calculation of the shortest cycle minus 19 are suggested to calculate the first fertile day in these circumstances. After charting for 6 to 12 months, take the earliest day resulting from the calculation of peak mucus day minus 6, or take the earliest day resulting from the calculation of the day of temperature minus 7. Both of these calculations should be cross-checked with the mucus symptom.

7

Natural family planning in special situations

At certain times in her life, a woman's fertility cycle may be interrupted by natural, and sometimes unnatural, events that demand a specific approach when viewed from the perspective of natural family planning. One of these natural interruptions to the cycle is pregnancy and childbirth, and it is important for a woman to know what is happening to her body and her fertility cycle during pregnancy and in the months following the birth of her child.

Another important and potentially stressful stage in a woman's life is the climacteric. This term is used to describe the period in a woman's life spanning the reproductive and non-reproductive years, and covers the separate stages of premenopause (when the reproductive cycle starts to slow down), the menopause (when the woman actually stops menstruating) and the postmenopause. During this time the woman has to cope with the decline and finally loss of her fertility. The more she knows about her body and what is happening to it at this time, the more chance she has of coming to terms with the changes and handling them successfully.

An unnatural event which completely disrupts the fertility cycle is the taking of contraceptive pills. Most contraceptive pills work by over-riding the natural hormonal pattern leading to ovulation. When a woman discontinues use of contraceptive pills it takes a while for her natural fertility cycle to reassert itself and for a regular pattern of ovulation to be re-established. Natural family planning techniques can help to reassure a woman that her natural fertility has been restored.

Returning fertility after childbirth

During pregnancy high levels of oestrogen and progesterone are produced which prevent the release of FSH and LH, thus suppressing ovulation. Added to these hormones in the bloodstream is another – prolactin – which is directly related to the production of milk for the nourishment of the child after it is born. This hormone also has a neutralising effect on FSH and LH to prevent ovulation occurring. These physiological blocks to ovulation therefore create a 'natural' infertility during pregnancy which spills over into the early weeks after the birth and sometimes lasts much longer.

The duration of this natural infertility after childbirth varies from woman to woman, but is directly related to whether the mother bottle feeds her baby, partially breast feeds, but supplements the baby's diet with other foods, or breast feeds on demand or what is called ecological breast feeding.

Fertility in the bottle-feeding mother
Within the first few weeks after delivery, the concentrations of oestrogen and progesterone in the mother's bloodstream fall. As the baby is not suckling from the breast, her body is not stimulated to produce prolactin, so the levels of this hormone also drop. As a result the physiological blocks to ovulation are removed and the period of natural infertility comes to an end.

There is no hard-and-fast rule for determining exactly when the bottle-feeding mother will return to fertility, though it is invariably before her breast-feeding sister. A study undertaken in 1968 of bottle-feeding mothers showed that all the women in the study had ovulated by the end of the fifth month after the birth; two-thirds had ovulated within three months of delivery and a few had ovulated within six weeks of delivery.

Natural family planning and the bottle-feeding mother
If a bottle-feeding mother wishes to avoid an unwanted pregnancy, she has to take into account the possibility of the fairly rapid return of her fertility and so recommence her observations and charting of fertility indicators as she did before the birth. A couple can be assured of infertility for the first three weeks after delivery and can therefore have sexual relations during this time if the woman feels well enough and enjoys it.

However, ideally the woman should start charting her BBT after 14 days, and certainly not later than the third week. In the beginning the BBT may be high or erratic but it should soon settle down. Although it will not warn her of the return of her fertility, the BBT will be useful in confirming any mucus symptoms she can detect. Once a definite temperature shift can be established to indicate ovulation, the woman can be assured that her normal fertility cycle is working again. If she has trouble observing her mucus because of a bloody vaginal discharge (called the lochial discharge), which appears after birth and may continue for six weeks or longer, it is advisable to postpone genital contact until the fourth high temperature after the temperature shift has been recorded. Then she can be sure that ovulation really has occurred and she is in the postovulatory infertile phase.

As soon as the lochial discharge dries up the woman can start charting her mucus pattern as before the birth to establish her basic pattern of infertility. If she perceives a pattern of dryness, the couple can have sexual intercourse in the evenings of alternate dry days following the rules for the mucus symptom in the preovulatory phase of the cycle.

If the woman detects a pattern of unchanging mucus, she should wait for two weeks to ensure that it really is a basic infertile pattern and not the first signs of the return of her fertility. Any change from dryness to mucus or from one type of mucus to another should be interpreted as a sign of returning fertility, and the couple should abstain from unprotected intercourse until the situation is clear. Thus, the last day of such mucus should be charted as the peak mucus symptom and fertility assumed for the following three days. This is where charting the BBT can be helpful, because a temperature shift can confirm the peak mucus symptom.

Generally, fertility returns fairly rapidly to the bottle-feeding mother and her cycles quickly return to normal ovulatory cycles, when the rules for observing and charting fertility indicators outlined in the previous chapters can be applied. If a woman wishes to use calendar calculations for detecting the beginning of the fertile phase once she has returned to regular cycles, she must begin to count a minimum of six cycle lengths anew. In the first cycles after childbirth, whether the mother breast feeds or bottle feeds, the luteal phase of the cycle (i.e. from ovulation to the following menstruation) tends to be shorter than usual, so that the whole cycle is shorter than she will normally experience. It is wise to ignore these shorter cycles when trying to work out calendar calculations, and to wait until the cycle pattern has stabilised before starting to record cycle lengths.

Fertility in the breast-feeding mother
For those women who are able to feed their babies naturally, breast feeding has many bonuses. Nutritionally, breast milk contains all the baby needs for the first six months of its life, including important antibodies to protect it from infection. The close physical contact with the mother during breast feeding cements the mother-infant bond so important to the baby, for whom touch and sight are the only possible channels of communication. The act of breast feeding is also psychologically fulfilling for the mother. On a more mundane level, breast feeding is a very economical and convenient method of feeding a baby.

For the mother who practises breast feeding on demand (called 'ecological' breast feeding) there is another advantage: the period of natural infertility that follows childbirth can be prolonged, sometimes for many months.

It is important to distinguish here between on-demand or ecological breast feeding and partial breast feeding, because in terms of infertility they are poles apart.

Ecological breast feeding means that the baby is encouraged to suckle not only for food but also for comfort. In such cases suckling occurs every two or three hours, day and night. Physiologically, whenever the baby suckles or stimulates the nipples, prolactin is produced, regardless of how much milk the baby actually consumes. After three or four hours the prolactin level drops again, but if the baby suckles often enough the high level of prolactin is maintained and ovulation prevented. In the Third World where this type of feeding regime is common and weaning does not take place until quite late in the infant's life, lactational infertility continues for two or even three years.

In *partial breast feeding*, on the other hand, the baby is fed at regular, well-spaced intervals and other liquids, such as sweetened water or fruit juices, or a dummy are given as 'comforters' between feeds. With this regime the prolactin levels are not maintained by frequent suckling and can drop low enough to allow the FSH and LH levels to increase. This results in ovulation, which can occur quite soon after the birth. Partial breast feeding obviously covers a wide variety of feeding regimes, depending on how often the baby feeds and on the number of supplementary feeds and their type, but in all cases fertility returns quickly.

As far as natural family planning is concerned, the advice to partially breast-feeding mothers is exactly the same as for the bottle-feeding mother. The first three weeks can be regarded as infertile, but after that observing and charting of fertility indicators has to be resumed, as fertility will return quite quickly, and the usual rules apply for the infertile and fertile times. It should also be noted that if ovulation has not occurred by the time the mother begins to wean her baby, it will occur almost immediately breast feeding is stopped.

Ecological breast feeding and natural infertility
Many excellent and detailed books about ecological breast feeding are available and it is unnecessary to go into detail here. (A list of books is included in the appendix.) What is important for the user of natural family planning methods is how long infertility lasts in women who breast feed their babies on demand, how to tell when fertility is returning and which indicators are the most useful for detecting this return.

Each woman's hormonal pattern is unique, and so too is the duration of her natural infertility. Consequently, even when feeding patterns are identical, fertility returns at varying times. Several factors can influence the duration of natural infertility including the type of suckling stimulus the baby offers the nipple, the quality of the mother's diet, whether or not she is under stress at any time while breast feeding, and when solid food is introduced into the baby's diet.

However, the three most important factors in predicting the return of fertility are:

1. The time of return of the menses.
2. The breastfeeding pattern.
3. The time that has elapsed since birth.

The time of return of the menses
There is a consensus among fertility researchers that any vaginal bleeding which occurs after the 56th day postpartum should be considered a return of 'menstruation' although the bleeding may not be recognized as the normal menstrual bleed by the woman. When this first bleed occurs early in the postpartum period, there is a high probability that it is an anovulatory bleed or, if preceded by an ovulation, this is in some manner defective followed by a deficient corpus luteum and an inadequate luteal phase. Either way, the probability of conception is markedly

reduced in such women. When the first bleed occurs after the first six months, it is more likely to be preceded by a normal ovulation, an adequate luteal phase and a higher probability of conception. Surveys have shown that the pregnancy rate in women who were amenorrhoeic during the first six months postpartum was less than 2% which compares favourably with current contraceptive usage.

The breastfeeding pattern
It is well recognized that a high suckling frequency and regular suckling both by day and night tends to prolong the natural lactational infertility. In contrast, long intervals between feeds whether by day or night, regular infant supplementation, or illness in either the mother or infant, tends to reduce the amount of suckling and promotes an earlier return to fertility. Normally satisfactory infant growth and development can be expected in the fully-breastfed infant for at least the first 4 to 6 months without additional supplements. If, however, the infant fails to thrive, the advice of a competent nutritionist/paediatrician should be sought and followed.

The time postpartum
In Western societies, the infant normally begins to receive additional foods at about 6 months of age. Intervals between breastfeeds become longer, the suckling duration and frequency diminish, and fertility returns within a matter of weeks or months. The later the resumption of fertility, the higher the chances of a normal ovulation and fertility preceding the first vaginal bleed.

On average, nevertheless, fertility does not return for 6 to 8 months in women who breastfeed unrestrictedly which is considerably longer than their bottle-feeding counterparts.

The breast-feeding mother should not wait for menstruation to herald the return of her fertility. It is quite possible for her to ovulate before the first menstruation after the birth and, unless she is alert to this and watching her fertility indicators, she may miss the occurrence of the first ovulation and become pregnant again before she wants to.

NFP charting during ecological breast feeding The most helpful indicator for the breast-feeding mother is her mucus pattern. This can indicate the continuation of her natural infertility, as well as providing a good early warning system for detecting the approach of fertility. In general, a woman need not chart her mucus pattern for the first five weeks after childbirth. At the end of five weeks the lochial discharge should have dried up and mucus observation can begin again.

Natural infertility can be expected to last for at least a few months in a woman who breast feeds on demand. Her first task, therefore, is to establish her basic infertile pattern, either of dryness, in which no mucus is felt or seen, or of unchanging mucus, in which unchanging infertile-type mucus is observed. When either of these patterns of infertility can be detected the rules for sexual intercourse are the same as those for the preovulatory infertile phase of a normal cycle; (cervical mucus method) in other words, the couple can have intercourse in the evenings of alternate dry days or days of unchanging mucus.

Where mucus changes suggest a possible return to fertility, or when vaginal bleeding occurs, the last mucus day, or the last day of spotting, should be treated as a possible peak mucus day and the following three days should be regarded as potentially fertile. Such a pattern is shown in Chart 15.

Some breast-feeding mothers will detect a basic infertile pattern of dampness and milky mucus. Here dry patches alternate with infertile-type and occasionally fertile-type mucus. This pattern is most commonly found in the later months of breast feeding, particularly if the mother has started to introduce solids into her baby's diet. Chart 16 shows such a pattern and it is obvious that unless the couple are prepared to accept long periods of abstinence from sexual intercourse, the mucus symptom must now be combined with another indicator of fertility.

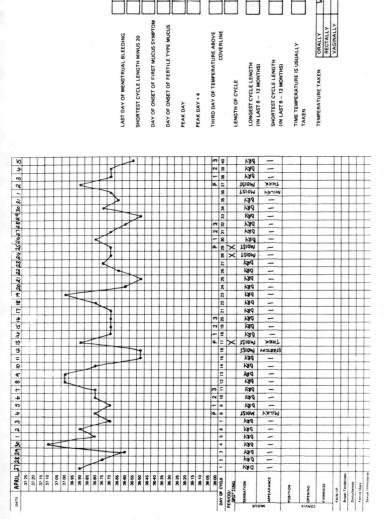

Chart 15 Basic infertile pattern of dryness following childbirth.

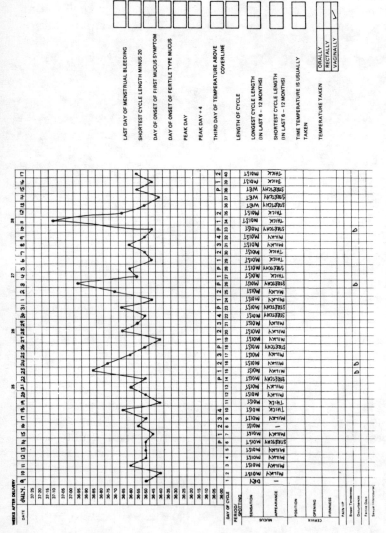

Chart 16 Basic infertile pattern during weaning.

Unfortunately, although the mucus symptom is very good for detecting the approach of fertility, it cannot distinguish between returning fertility and imminent ovulation. If a mother weans her baby slowly, the mucus symptom may indicate a long phase of possible fertility before ovulation actually occurs. Retrospectively, it is possible to see that abstinence was not necessary, but this cannot be predicted from the mucus symptom.

This is where the changes in the cervix can provide the vital back-up information for distinguishing between possible fertility and impending ovulation, because progressive changes in the cervix do not occur until ovulation is close.

The breast-feeding mother should observe and chart the changes in her cervix in exactly the same way as for a normal cycle. During the early weeks after delivery the cervix will not have returned completely to its prepregnant state, but by the twelfth week it should have returned to normal. However, it must be remembered that once a woman has had a child the cervical os will not close as completely as it did before, though she will still be able to detect a sufficient change in the width of the os to distinguish between the fertile and infertile states. Once the mucus symptom has indicated a possible return to fertility, the breast-feeding mother can use the changes in her cervix to detect the approach of ovulation.

As changes in the cervix are a more precise indicator of impending ovulation, we advise all women to gain experience in detecting and charting cervical changes during their normal fertile cycles, so that when they require a double-check indicator for returning fertility after child-birth they know exactly what to expect and look for.

Finally, the BBT is not a very helpful indicator during the period of natural infertility, as it usually presents an erratic and uninterpretable pattern if charted. However, at the approach of returning fertility, the BBT pattern begins to settle and stabilize at a lower level. This is an additional sign which helps to confirm the predictive signals in the cervix and the mucus. In addition, the temperature shift is a very useful and necessary confirmation that ovulation has actually occurred for the first time since delivery. So charting of the BBT should begin as soon as:

1 Any vaginal bleeding occurs, because this may be a forerunner to ovulation.
2 The mucus shows any signs of returning fertility; in other words, if patches of fertile-type mucus are detected, or if there is a change in the basic infertile pattern of dryness, since this may indicate impending ovulation.
3 If the suckling regime is altered suddenly, say by illness in the mother or the baby, which could lead to a rapid return of fertility.

In summary, the mother who breast feeds her baby on an unrestricted basis can anticipate an extended period of natural infertility after childbirth. This infertility is normally easily detected by the pattern of cervical mucus. However, her fertility may begin to return some weeks before ovulation actually occurs, and in this case changes in the cervix will provide assistance in interpreting ambiguous mucus symptoms.

The climacteric

Just as puberty, when reproductive life is beginning, is a time of physical and psychological adjustment for the teenager, so the climacteric, when a woman's reproductive life is 'ending', is a time of readjustment for a woman to her new status.

Until recently, this time in a woman's life was poorly understood and even more poorly catered for, most of her symptoms being written off as consequences of the 'change', for which apparently nothing could be done. Over the last decade the physiology of the climacteric has become better known, if not yet fully understood. This has led to a new perception and awareness of the climacteric and its concomitant problems, with advantageous repercussions for women in this process of adaptation.

It is difficult to set an age to the climacteric. Alarming as it may sound, the ageing process with declining fertility begins at about 30 years of age and continues to infertility after the menopause, when menstrual periods cease, around the age of 50–51. In general, the climacteric occurs between the ages of 45 and 54, though it can happen earlier or later for some women.

As with all life's stages, for some women the climacteric poses no problems; 20% of women sail through this period and reach the menopause before they are even aware it has begun. Other women experience all sorts of problems and have a very stormy passage through these years.

What happens to a woman's body during the climacteric?
During the reproductive years the female hormones, oestrogen and progesterone, are secreted as a result of the growth and release of an ovum in monthly cycles, under the influence of FSH and LH from the pituitary gland. During the climacteric there is a progressive decline and failure of this mechanism until finally, at and after the menopause, no further ova mature or are released.

Why should this failure occur in a woman who has many years of life before her? Is it the result of a failure in the production of LH and FSH? Or is it a failure of the ovary and follicles to respond to this hormonal stimulus? Extensive research into the pituitary hormones shows that, far from falling, increased secretions of FSH and LH are poured into the woman's bloodstream during the climacteric. The failure, therefore, must lie in a lack of response in the ovaries. An old explanation for this was that the store of immature ova, with which every woman is born, was now exhausted. However, research has shown this view to be invalid. It is still not known why the follicles show a declining response to the hormonal stimulus during the climacteric, or why they finally fail to respond at all at and after the menopause.

101

This gradual failure of the follicles to respond to the pituitary hormones does, however, mean that the cyclical supply of oestrogen and progesterone is also interrupted. A woman may experience several physical symptoms as her body adjusts to this often rapid decline in the hormonal supply.

Symptoms of the climacteric
Several signs indicate the diminishing hormonal levels in the woman's body.

1   Due to the erratic response of the follicles in the ovary to FSH stimulation, irregular cycles, where previously they have been regular, are usually the first and most common indication of the arrival of the climacteric. These can vary from short ones of 23 days to long cycles of 50–60 days. In the long cycles, the follicular phase is prolonged; after ovulation the luteal phase may be of normal length suggesting a truly fertile cycle or it may be short (BBT shift-menstruation less than 8 days) suggesting a defective ovulation and corpus luteum and, as a consequence, a subfertile or perhaps an infertile cycle.

In contrast, in the very short cycle, the follicle responds unusually rapidly to the FSH stimulation and a normal ovulation can occur as early as day 6 of the cycle, followed by a normal luteal phase. Such cycles are apparently fertile and pose a problem in that one cannot predict at menstruation that ovulation is going to occur early. The NFP rules have to be adapted to accomodate both the long and the short cycles. (See NFP and the climacteric.)

2   Anovulatory cycles, or cycles in which ovulation does not occur, so that the entire cycle is infertile. The woman may still menstruate but this is, in fact, a withdrawal bleed (due to a drop in oestrogen) rather than a proper period.

3   The production of fertile-type mucus by the cervix is markedly reduced and only secreted by the upper

crypts of the cervical canal. The scanty amount of mucus and the fact that it has to come first through the length of the cervical canal, to arrive at the cervical opening; from there it has to pass down through the vagina to be perceived at the vulva. As a result, in practice, many premenopausal women find that their mucus discharge is very scanty, with the fertile mucus only appearing for ½ to 1 day before the BBT shift; other women in apparently ovulatory cycles never experience any fertile-type mucus at the vulva despite a distinct BBT shift and a normal length luteal phase. Such women should look for the fertile mucus at the cervix in addition to noting the cervical changes during the fertile phase.

4   Breakthrough bleeding is more common during the climacteric than at any other time in a woman's reproductive life. This may occur as spotting or even a few days of heavier bleeding resembling a period, but in this instance it indicates a highly fertile time in the cycle. The woman may also have irregular spotting or bleeding right through the cycle showing that the follicular growth and therefore the levels of oestrogen and progesterone, are erratic, thus causing irregular growth in the lining of the uterus. When the corpus luteum produces less than normal amounts of progesterone, a woman may also experience premenstrual shedding (vaginal spotting occurring one or several days before menstruation). This occurs because there is insufficient progesterone to 'hold' the lining of the uterus, which consequently begins to shed earlier than it would normally. If the woman is keeping a temperature chart, she will notice that her temperature remains on the high phase during the shedding, only dropping when the actual menstrual bleeding starts.

5   Some women experience quite severe pain and tenderness in their breasts as a result of the very high levels of oestrogen required to trigger ovulation in the resistant ovaries. Where ovulation is delayed these symptoms

may persist for long periods and be very distressing.

6   Hot flushes are, perhaps, the most well-known sign of the climacteric, although they do not occur in all women. They are sudden flashes of heat, especially around the head and neck, and are believed to be caused by the decreasing levels of oestrogen. They are usually an early sign of the climacteric and diminishing fertility. Hot flushes can occur at any time, day or night, and often cause insomnia, tiredness and irritability in the sufferer.

For those women using natural methods of family planning, hot flushes offer an additional indicator of infertility, because they occur as a consequence of low oestrogen levels.

7   Another common symptom of the climacteric is an increasing dryness in the vagina, again caused by the diminishing levels of oestrogen. This may make sexual intercourse painful for the woman, though a substitute for the missing lubrication, such as KY jelly, can be helpful.

Psychological and social problems associated with the climacteric

As in puberty, when sudden erratic increasing concentrations of sex steroid hormones cause both clinical and psychological problems for adolescents, the rapid hormonal changes in premenopausal women often result in behavioural and psychological problems, in addition to the clinical symptoms related to the drop in concentration of the sex hormones. There are also external factors related to this life stage which aggravate or interact with the hormone-related clinical symptoms.

Most women fear aging and its likely effect on appearance and attractiveness to the partner; the youth culture of today's society only serves to increase this fear. A further factor is the lack or loss of a career which is more profoundly felt at this time of life by those women who have spent the greater part of their lives caring for their family. The 'empty-nest syndrome' is a very tangible reality during the premenopause stage, often resulting in the woman suffering a feeling of worthlessness or not being needed by anybody. It is often difficult to disentangle the psychological from the clinical symptoms and, to some extent, both are intertwined in all premenopausal women presenting these symptoms.

Osteoporosis and the climacteric

Osteoporosis ('brittle bones') is a condition where the bone mass is so reduced that as a consequence the bones break (fracture) more easily. As with all bodily cells, from infancy onwards, bone cells are destroyed and new cells formed. During childhood and adolescence, there is a natural increase in bone mass due to the stimulus of the growth hormone and the continuous use of bones in walking, standing and exercise. Nevertheless, without an adequate diet and especially one that provides sufficient calcium, the influence of growth and exercise is constrained and normal bone architecture is not attained. The deposition of calcium in bone tissue, which is essential for the formation of an adequate bone mass, depends on several hormones of which oestrogen is one.

As a result of decreasing concentrations of oestrogen at the menopause, there is an increased rate of bone loss which may in some women lead to osteoporosis. Not all women get osteoporosis, however, and there are traditional and well-known risk factors for women who do develop the condition:

1 A diet inadequate in calcium during childhood and adolescence.
2 A sedentary life style.
3 A family history of osteoporosis.
4 Being Caucasian or Asian. (The condition is rare in women of Afro-Caribbean origin.)
5 Low body weight.

6 Smoking cigarettes.
7 A high alcohol intake.
8 Drug abuse.

The administration of oestrogen (hormone replacement therapy, HRT) has attained great prominence in the prevention of osteoporosis. Oestrogens have been shown to delay bone loss, but a minimum of five years' oestrogen therapy is required to reduce the fracture frequency. One of the difficulties is in selecting those women who require HRT. It is also recognized that, on terminating the oestrogen therapy, bone is lost at a similar rate to that of the immediate post-menopausal phase; this makes it difficult to know when to stop the oestrogen therapy. Furthermore, such treatment is not without adverse risks in other ways (cancer of the lining of the womb and breast cancer are the most important complications); one must also accept that although studies have shown that oestrogen therapy can limit post-menopausal bone loss, it cannot replace the loss of bone mass resulting from deficiencies in early life. It is also true that regular exercise and a diet containing an adequate calcium intake are effective in conserving post-menopausal bone loss and have no adverse side effects. Tiludronate, a new biphosphonate compound which inhibits bone loss due to disease in younger persons, has recently been recommended as a safer alternative to HRT.

A diet low in salt also helps to conserve calcium in bone and helps to prevent osteoporosis.

Hormone replacement therapy during the climacteric and afterwards
Symptoms of the climacteric are dependent on several factors, some of which are independent of declining ovarian function and reduced levels of oestrogen and progesterone, e.g. psychological and social factors. It follows, therefore, that hormone replacement will not always cure all the symptoms and neither is the therapy without its risks. Oestrogen has a profound and widespread effect on the whole body and there is a well-

known connection between taking oestrogen and cancer of the endometrium (lining of the womb). In an effort to counteract this complication of oestrogen treatment, progesterone is always given with the oestrogen unless the womb has been previously taken out (hysterectomy). The progesterone produces feelings of nausea and bloatedness in many women; in addition, the hormones are stopped each month to allow a bleed to clear the lining of the womb. Women may not like the idea of having regular monthly periods at and after the menopause. The doses of oestrogen may also increase the risk of breast cancer. Certainly HRT does alleviate the hot flushes and the night sweats and, as already stated, it helps to reduce the increased bone loss that occurs at this time of life leading to osteoporosis.

However, nature ensures that, after a transition period, a steady amount of oestrogen is released into the blood stream, arguably the correct amount for a woman at this stage of her life. During the reproductive years a woman gets 90% of her oestrogen from the ovaries. The remaining 10% is produced by the conversion of androgen (male hormone) which is secreted in small amounts by the ovaries, to oestrogen. When ovarian activity has ceased during the climacteric, the ovaries produce little or no oestrogen but continue to produce androgen. The oestrogen derived from the conversion of this androgen and that secreted by the adrenal glands maintains a fairly stable level of oestrogen in the bloodstream, although at a lower concentration than before the menopause. With the production of this 'new' oestrogen, the hot flushes disappear. The hot flushes and the irregular cycles can, therefore, be viewed as the body's initial reaction to the new situation, a transition phase until the body has adapted to the third epoch in the woman's life.

Since psycho-social factors produce many of the signs and symptoms of the climacteric, one should remember that, in some cases, a sympathetic understanding may be more helpful to the individual woman than continuous doses of hormones. One may also question whether the continued administration of oestrogen and progesterone will depress the natural mechanisms whereby an amount of oestrogen suitable for the metabolism at this stage of life is produced? Should this happen, does the process only begin when the replacement hormones are withdrawn? Or is the natural mechanism completely depressed for life as may happen in early years with the pituitary gland?

Natural family planning and the climacteric
The climacteric is a period of declining fertility. The probability of conception where no method of contraception is used varies from 80–90% in young women, 40–50% at the age of forty, 10–20% at forty-five to a figure of 0–5% at the age of fifty. Thus the chances of pregnancy are very much reduced for those women who use NFP at this time of their life.

As the woman's fertility is waning at this stage in her life, so too are the signs and symptoms of fertility that she can observe. Her charts will show increasing evidence of infertility, and the key to successful application of natural family planning methods is not so much determining the fertile phase, as being able to make positive identification of infertility.

The interpretation of the charts throughout this period may be complicated by irregular cycles, poor temperature shifts, scanty mucus and short postovulatory phases. However, providing women are given the necessary physiological knowledge about the climacteric and have previous experience at charting, they manage to continue the interpretation of their charts without any great difficulty.

A fairly common problem with charting during the climacteric is the long cycle. Such a cycle is illustrated in Chart 17. Here it is obvious from observations of a lack of mucus that, following menstruation, the ovaries are in a state of non-activity. Women in the climacteric will be much more aware of this feeling of positive dryness than they were in previous years, and it provides a useful indication of infertility. In Chart 17 the sensation of dryness continues for 30 days, with mucus appearing

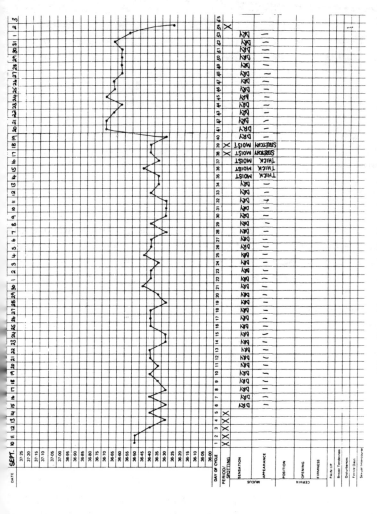

Chart 17 A long cycle during the climacteric.

for the first time in the cycle on day 35. For the next five days there is a normal build-up of mucus with distinctly fertile-type mucus observed on days 38 and 39. This is also accompanied by spotting. There is a rapid reversion to dryness on day 40 and a clear temperature shift on day 41, indicating that ovulation has occurred.

The end of the fertile phase is clearly evident. Being confident about the duration of the preovulatory infertile phase is more of a problem, given its length. This particular woman was practising the double-check method, using calendar calculations combined with the mucus symptom to detect the beginning of the fertile phase. Her shortest cycle over the last 12 months was 27 days, so using the calendar calculation shortest cycle minus 19, fertility, and therefore abstinence, is predicted to begin on day 8. In retrospect, the chart reveals this to be incorrect. Since this woman is 47 years old and this long cycle probably indicates the beginning of the climacteric, the calendar calculation is obviously no longer of much use. Instead, she chose to combine the mucus symptom, following the rule of intercourse on alternate dry days, with examination of her cervix to identify when ovulation was about to occur. By doing this, future long cycles presented no problems as she was able positively to identify her increasing periods of infertility.

The occurrence of an early ovulation, often on day 6 of the cycle, poses an even greater difficulty for women than the long cycle. This is because sexual intercourse in the first days of the cycle, even during menstruation, could result in conception, and most conceptions in the premenopause occur between days 1 to 6 in such short cycles. The rules for the premenopausal woman have to be adapted to accommodate the possibility of such an early ovulation, so during the premenopause all vaginal bleeding, even true menstrual bleeding, is considered to be fertile. The last day of menstrual bleeding is deemed a peak fertility day while the following four days are potentially fertile. Where a pregnancy is not desired, abstinence is practised from the onset of menstruation until the evening of the 4th day after the peak (bleeding) day. If dryness occurs in the days following bleeding, a long cycle can be anticipated and the rules as given for a long cycle are followed. If cervical mucus or changes in the cervix are noted in the post-menstrual days, one can expect an early ovulation and abstinence is advised until after the peak mucus day and the BBT shift as in the normal cycle.

Menopause
Menopause is the stage at which menstruation stops completely. With irregular cycles such as those experienced during the climacteric it is sometimes difficult for a woman to tell whether a menstruation will be the last one. However, it is generally accepted that if a woman has not menstruated for six months, it is unlikely that she will do so again. Certainly, if a woman experiences any vaginal bleeding more than one year from her last menstruation she should seek medical advice, because it is improbable that it is a normal menstruation.

Natural family planning after stopping the contraceptive pill

Many women who seek advice on natural family planning methods have been previously taking the contraceptive pill. Some stop taking the pill because they are concerned about its possible side-effects, some wish to 'take a rest' from the pill, and others stop because they wish to have a child. Whatever the reason, the first step is to monitor their fertility over a few cycles using the usual natural indicators. This ensures that their natural cycles have reasserted themselves and that their bodily systems have returned to normal – a particularly important point for those women embarking on a pregnancy.

Since there are at least 33 different varieties of the oral contraceptive pill, and its effect varies from woman to woman, it is extremely difficult to predict how and when fertility will return in any individual woman.

By its action of suppressing ovulation, the pill makes the body believe that it is pregnant – a long-term pregnancy extending over years rather than months. Different pills have different actions but all kinds have one or more of the following effects:

1   The carefully balanced feedback system of hormones to the pituitary is blocked by the continuous high doses of oestrogen and progesterone in the bloodstream, so ovulation does not take place.
2   The cervical mucus is maintained in a constant state of 'hostility' to the sperm.
3   The endometrial lining of the uterus is also maintained in a 'hostile' state, inhibiting the implantation of a fertilised ovum.

How long a woman remains infertile after discontinuing the pill depends on how quickly her hormonal system recovers and responds to the new low levels of oestrogen and progesterone and restarts production of FSH and LH. In general, there is little delay but in some cases the first menstruation after stopping the pill may not occur for up to 90 days, especially if the woman has been taking the combined pill (oestrogen and progesterone). It is important for women stopping the pill to be aware of the possibility of a delay in the return of their fertility, or anxieties about potential sterility may further slow the process.

Pills which work by changing the nature of the cervical mucus and lining of the uterus – the mini or progesterone-only pills – have little effect on the pituitary and so fertility returns much more rapidly to women using these than to those taking combined pills.

Charting for the post-pill woman
The first cycle after stopping the pill is the one most likely to cause problems. If the woman can ride out this time, the following cycles should have returned to normal and she should have no problems applying natural family planning methods.

The main hurdle for a woman stopping the pill, and so charting her fertility cycles for the first time, is inexperience at reading the natural signs and symptoms of fertility. This is compounded by the fact that the cycles immediately after stopping the pill may show irregularities that will disappear once her system has settled down again.

The basal body temperature   It is important for women stopping the pill to start charting their BBT because this provides one of the best objective signs that ovulation has occurred and fertility returned. It is also fairly easy for women to learn to measure and chart this particular symptom of fertility.

However, BBT can only indicate when ovulation has occurred and is therefore not helpful in predicting the approach of fertility. This can be a problem if ovulation is delayed and the preovulatory phase extends over several weeks. In such cases, as for women after childbirth and approaching the menopause, it is best to observe and chart another indicator of fertility in conjunction with the temperature. Even so, it is advisable for couples to abstain from sexual intercourse for the first cycle after stopping the pill until after the temperature shift, because inexperience at observing and charting all the symptoms of fertility may lead to misinterpretation and an unplanned pregnancy.

The mucus symptom   The usual rules for learning to observe the mucus symptom apply to women stopping the pill. For the first cycle sexual intercourse should be avoided until the fourth day after the temperature shift. This helps to prevent any confusion between mucus secretions and seminal fluid during the early infertile phase and offers the woman the chance to become familiar with her own mucus pattern.

It may be that in this first cycle the body will make several attempts at ovulation before it actually succeeds. This rise and fall in the levels of oestrogen and progesterone will be reflected in the mucus pattern, showing infertile-type mucus followed by fertile-type mucus followed by infertile-type mucus again.

Also, it is possible in this first post-pill cycle for the woman to observe a continuous, often fairly heavy mucus discharge from the beginning of the cycle, which persists for some weeks. This discharge is often caused by a cervical erosion or abrasion, which is common in women who are taking or who have taken the contraceptive pill. Alternatively, the woman's body may have stored the excess oestrogen from the pill, and this has to be eliminated from her body slowly over a few weeks or even months. In this case the mucus pattern obviously bears no relation to the growth and release of an ovum. These problems, combined with the fact that it takes at least three cycles to be confident about detecting the mucus peak, mean that observing and recording the mucus symptom may be a rather frustrating and unreliable exercise for the first few cycles. However, once the irregularities have disappeared, normal observation and charting can begin and the usual rules for the mucus method of natural family planning apply.

Changes in the cervix As with the mucus symptom, the disadvantage of this indicator is the learning phase necessary before the woman can be confident of correctly interpreting the cervical changes. On average it takes about three months to become really familiar with changes in the cervix and so it cannot be relied on in the first few cycles after stopping the pill. However, once a woman has learnt to observe and chart this symptom the usual rules can be applied.

Minor indicators It is quite common for mid-cycle spotting or bleeding to occur around the time of the first ovulation in post-pill women. This can be used to confirm a peak mucus symptom, if this is detectable, or a temperature shift. Also, many women experience ovulation pain during this first ovulation after the pill, and this can be used as a back-up.

114

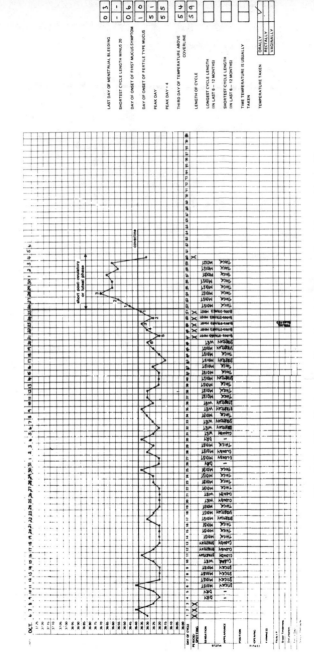

Chart 18 The first cycle after stopping the oral contraceptive pill.

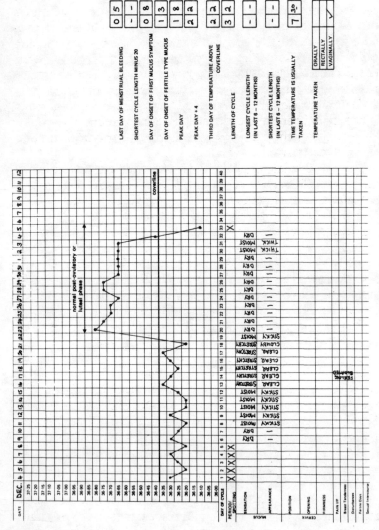

Chart 19 The second cycle after stopping the oral contraceptive pill.

Charts 18 and 19 show the first two cycles for a woman who had taken the combined contraceptive pill for four years. In Chart 18 the first day of the cycle is the first day of bleeding after stopping the pill. This bleeding is not a proper menstruation but a withdrawal bleed as a consequence of the drop in oestrogen after stopping the pill. The mucus pattern apparent in Chart 18 shows that the body made several attempts to ovulate before finally achieving it on day 51 of the cycle. The temperature shift from low phase temperatures to high phase temperatures is clearly evident and confirms the peak mucus symptom. Mid-cycle spotting provides an extra confirmatory indicator of ovulation.

The postovulatory phase in this cycle is very short, with menstruation occurring on day 60 of the cycle. This chart, therefore, shows many of the irregularities that may occur in the first cycle after stopping the pill.

It also shows the reasons why it is important to abstain from sexual intercourse during the pre-ovulatory phase. Although ovulation does not occur until day 51, the mucus pattern indicates several potentially fertile days earlier in the cycle as the oestrogen levels rise in an attempt to trigger ovulation. The postovulatory phase is very short, limiting the infertile days when intercourse would be safe. One of the main problems for women stopping the pill and their partners is the modification necessary in their sexual behaviour. The couple have been used to having sexual intercourse whenever they desired, whereas the first cycle after stopping the pill demands abstinence for a potentially long period until the woman's body has settled down and her normal fertility cycle has re-established itself.

In Chart 19 the woman's cycles have returned almost to normal, except that the cycle is still fairly long. Both the peak mucus symptom and the temperature shift are clearly evident and the postovulatory phase has also returned to normal, allowing the woman and her partner a reasonable number of days for sexual intercourse without risk. After two cycles of observation and charting, this woman can be confident that her natural menstrual cycles have resumed, and she can begin to apply the rules for normal ovulatory cycles.

Post-pill pregnancy

If a woman has stopped taking the contraceptive pill because she and her partner have decided to have a child, it is important that they wait for three or four cycles before attempting conception. This ensures that her body has had time to return to its normal fertile state and has eliminated the effects of unnatural hormonal fluctuations. Following the rules for the peak mucus symptom, the couple can then optimise their chances of conceiving by having sexual intercourse as near as possible to the peak mucus day.

Natural family planning methods are also useful here, because they show with great precision when fertilisation has occurred, which is very helpful for monitoring the progress of the pregnancy and eliminates the problem of doubtful dates.

8

Natural family planning and achieving pregnancy

Infertility

The term 'Family Planning' supposes the ability of a couple to achieve or avoid a pregnancy according to their family planning intentions. This ability to conceive has to be the most important factor since, where a couple is unable to do so, there is an urgent need for family planning. At least a quarter of the people who come to natural family planning clinics are seeking advice about natural methods, not for the purposes of birth control, but to help them overcome difficulties in conceiving.

With the modern emphasis on limiting family size and the freedom to choose not to have children at all, the plight of this increasingly large number of couples who have problems in achieving pregnancy is often overlooked. It is estimated that more than 10% of couples in Western countries experience problems of infertility. The number of subfertile couples – those who take longer than usual to achieve a pregnancy – is probably even greater, but as many never seek help, it is difficult to determine an accurate figure.

Many of these couples *can* be helped by a natural approach to family planning. Learning about fertility awareness and the methods for pinpointing the peak fertile time in a cycle enables these couples to time intercourse to coincide with ovulation and so maximise the potential for conception in that cycle. This really quite simple advice can often prove invaluable. Infertility obviously causes a great deal of anxiety, distress and sometimes feelings of guilt in the couple affected; the psychological support, understanding and reassurance offered by the NFP teacher can also be extremely helpful in allaying the couple's fears, and developing a positive approach to the problem.

It is important, therefore, that a book about family planning addresses this problem so that Natural Family Planning teachers and clinics can offer informed and sympathetic advice to infertile couples seeking help.

What is infertility?
The term 'involuntary infertility' is applied to couples who are unable to achieve a pregnancy after approximately one year of regular sexual intercourse without contraceptives. Normally, 80 per cent of couples who are trying to have a baby will conceive within 12 months. However, it is important to point out that having intercourse without contraceptives does not necessarily result in an instant pregnancy. Many couples are often unnecessarily anxious about the delay in conceiving and this stress can be counter-productive, throwing the woman's hormonal system off balance, actually inhibiting ovulation and so exacerbating the problem.

For many decades, infertility was seen as a social stigma and couples were reluctant to come forward for advice and treatment. Moreover, when treatment was considered, the woman was generally the person to be investigated, nobody ever suggesting that the male might be the infertile partner. Happily, these attitudes are changing thanks to a better understanding of both the male and female reproductive physiology and leading to a more efficient diagnosis than was possible some years back.

Notwithstanding, some causes are, as yet, poorly understood or not yet amenable to treatment; it is essential to inform such couples about the limitations of medicine so that they will not be too disappointed later if they are not successful. NFP teachers should be sensitive to the feelings of the couples and realise the anxiety and stress under which many live continuously. Tact and understanding are necessary when giving counsel and advice.

The causes of infertility
From our knowledge of reproductive physiology, we know that fertility depends on the possibility of a fertilizing sperm and a mature ovum meeting and fusing. Any condition, therefore, where either of these sex cells are not quantitatively or qualitatively normal or prevented from fusing in the outer end of the fallopian tube will cause infertility in varying degrees.

The cause of infertility can be in the male, the female or partly in both partners. Studies suggest that a male factor occurs in 25 per cent, a female factor is present in 40 per cent and both male and female factors are present in between 30–40 per cent.

The causes of infertility and subfertility in the UK presented at a Conference in 1987 were as follows:

21 per cent suffered from ovulatory failure
14 per cent had tubal damage
24 per cent resulted from sperm defect or dysfunction
28 per cent no cause was found for the infertility after investigation. This subgroup of 28 per cent who showed an unexplained infertility are particularly likely to benefit from the information and advice given by the NFP teacher.

Medically, we can subdivide both male and female infertility into:

A   Primary infertility, where the couple have never succeeded in conceiving.
B   Secondary infertility, where the couple have conceived one or more times but have difficulty in conceiving again.

Male causes of infertility

1 *Azoospermia* is a condition in which no sperms are produced by the testes. This is a rare condition associated with undescended testicle, abnormalities of the testes or the epididymus, normally resulting from the occurrence of viral infections such as mumps which damage the testes, or from taking cytotoxic drugs, or radiation therapy to the lower abdomen for the treatment of cancers of the lymph nodes and the testes. There is no successful treatment in this group.

2 *Oligospermia* is a condition in which, although they are produced, sperm are deficient either in number or quality or both in comparison with those in the normal ejaculate and is, on the contrary, a relatively common occurrence. Normally, the 2cc ejaculate contains around 400 million sperm, of which a high percentage are motile and normal. While it is difficult to classify sperm counts precisely, it is generally held that a sperm count of 60 million or less would constitute oligospermia. An ejaculate containing between 60 and 400 million sperm is a grey area which is sometimes associated with subfertility, although not necessarily so.

We require much more accurate information on the relationship of the number and quality of sperms and subsequent infertility and subfertility before the prognosis can be based on the actual number of sperm.

Causes associated with the condition of oligospermia are:
   (a) Injury, infections or operations in the genital area.
   (b) A varicocele (varicose vein) around the testes. This acts by increasing the heat in the area of the testes which adversely affects the production of sperm. Removal of the varicocele may often dramatically restore fertility.
   (c) Other sources of overheating in the region of the testes such as excessive hot baths, gross obesity, tight underpants, long hours of sedentary work

(long distance lorrydrivers), may also be a cause of oligospermia.

(d) Cigarette smoking (over 20 per day) can reduce the number and motility of the sperm.

(e) Excessive alcohol reduces both the production of sperm and the hormone testosterone. It also decreases libido which may aggravate the infertility or subfertility.

(f) Deficiencies in seminal fluid may cause immotility of the sperm even when the number is adequate.

(g) Fatigue often decreases libido.

(h) Very frequent sexual intercourse can lead to a situation where the demand exceeds the supply. In addition, subfertility or infertility is associated with a high percentage of abnormal sperms even where sperm numbers are normal.

3   The progress in medical technology has enabled specialists to distinguish two types of sperm antibodies:

(a) *Male auto-antibodies.* These are produced by the testes and deactivate the sperms by causing them to clump together. Their presence is known by a special test to examine the ejaculate and seminal fluid.

(b) *Female antisperm antibodies (spermagglutinins).* These may be present in the cervical mucus and cause immobilization of the sperms at the level of the cervix, which prevents further progress of the sperm towards the fallopian tubes. The diagnosis of this condition can be made by performing a special test (sperm invasion or sperm penetration) where sperm and mucus are brought into contact on a slide and progressive movement is seen and measured by microscopic observation.

4   *Psychosexual causes.* Impotence, premature ejaculation, non-consummation and defective coital technique can cause infertility or subfertility. These factors often have a psychological background and can be caused

by the couple rather than one partner.

The exception is that of impotence caused by fatigue, debility, drugs or neurological defects consequent on spinal injuries or diseases.

Screening tests

Initial investigations, such as a sperm count or a postcoital test where the presence and motility of the sperm within the mucus after sexual intercourse are assessed, can easily be carried out through cooperation between the NFP teacher and the general practitioner. At least three such tests should be done before sending the man for specialist investigation. If the test results are normal a male cause can generally be excluded.

It is important to know that the prognostic value of the postcoital test is much better than that of seminal fluid counts. However, to be accurate, the presence of good quality mucus is essential; the NFP teacher is ideally placed to advise the couple on the proper time for intercourse in the presence of good mucus. Very often specialists forget to tell couples about this, so the couple should always be aware of its importance.

Treatment of male infertility

If a cause can be found, treatment is generally best carried out in a specialist clinic. However, at best, the treatment of male infertility is not very successful and one can expect low conception rates where the cause is the male factor.

Recently, the treatment of males with hormones has been tried although without much success. The best results to date have been obtained by the technique of Gamete Intratubal Transfer (GIFT). For this technique see page 138.

In all cases, however, the NFP teacher must give support and encouragement to the couple while not losing sight of possible underlying causes and available treatment and their limitations.

Artificial Insemination

Artificial insemination is the term used when sperm from either the husband or a donor is placed within the uterine cavity.

Artificial Insemination Husband (AIH) is sometimes done where the number of sperm in the ejaculate is small or where the cervical mucus is hostile to the sperm (spermagglutinins). The success rate for fertilization and pregnancy using this technique is very poor.

Artificial Insemination Donor (AID)

When the husband or partner's sperms are deficient and the woman wants to conceive, sperm obtained from donor men can be injected into the uterus through the cervix during the fertile phase of the cycle.

The sperm used can be fresh (obtained by masturbation) or frozen in sperm banks for varying periods of time. Some attempt is made to 'match' the physical characteristics of the donor with the husband or partner. However, the identity of the father cannot be disclosed and, if pregnancy results, the child has no right or possibility of knowing who his/her biological father is.

Female factors in infertility and subfertility

In general, there are four possible causes for female infertility and subfertility.

Menstrual/Ovulation disorders
Utero/cervical causes
Psychosexual problems in the partnership
Tubal problems

1 *Menstrual/Ovulation disorders*
A normal menstrual cycle varies between 25 and 35 days with an ovulation occurring between 10 and 16 days before the end of the cycle. At the time of the menarche and the premenopause the cycle lengths vary between 21 and 90 days. Between the ages of 20 and 40 years the menstrual cycle becomes stabilized at

normal lengths, and cyclical ovulation becomes more regularly established as the hypothalamic/pituitary system develops and matures. In some women, however, full maturation of the system is never achieved and these women continue with irregular cycles for the rest of their lives. Ovulation is not only erratic in this group, but the number of ovulations per calendar year is also reduced and these women can often be diagnosed infertile or subfertile. Even in established ovulators, stress and emotional upsets can delay, or occasionally accelerate, the development of a follicle, resulting in a cycle longer or shorter than usual.

Women who keep a symptothermal chart usually have a fairly clear picture of their fertility status and initial screening of both subfertile and infertile women can be done both economically and satisfactorily by the NFP clinic and teacher. Where women are found to have scanty, deficient or absent ovulations, the teacher will then refer them to a specialist clinic. This ensures that a number of subfertile women are spared the stress of lengthy and unnecessary hormonal and ultrasound examinations.

A *Anovulatory cycles.* In these cycles the egg follicle does not develop fully and the ovum is not released from the ovary. When a young woman has no menstruation (amenorrhoea), one may reasonably suspect anovulation, provided other causes, such as pregnancy, are excluded.

There are several possible causes for the occurrence of anovulatory cycles with the following being the most common causes.

(a) A congenital absence of primary egg follicles in the ovaries is an uncommon cause, but when it does occur the condition is untreatable. More commonly, anovulation is due to a deficiency of the hormones FSH and LH from the pituitary or a deficiency of the FSH and LH releasing factors from the hypothalamus.

(b) For women in the 20 to 40 age group, this type of anovulatory cycle may be due to the effects of taking the oral contraceptive pill and the condition may persist for as long as two years or more after discontinuing the pill in some women.

(c) Another cause is the presence in the circulation of high levels of the hormone prolactin. This condition of hyperprolactaemia may result from a tumour of the pituitary gland which secretes too much prolactin, or it may be caused by a deficiency of the inhibiting mechanism from the hypothalamus which is not able to restrain the amounts of prolactin getting into the blood stream.

(d) A similar mechanism operates in women who have difficulty in establishing regular ovulatory cycles after breastfeeding. In these women the hypothalamic mechanism does not return to normal quickly and one finds that some have high levels of prolactin in blood samples.

The diagnosis of ovulatory disorders. As stated previously, a good menstrual history and examination of symptothermal chart can be an excellent screening method for ovulatory disorders. If anything abnormal is suspected, a detailed hormonal and ultrasonic examination should be carried out. Occasionally, an ovarian biopsy is necessary to establish a congenital absence of primary follicles.

Treatment. When the cause is a deficiency of the hypothalamic or pituitary hormones, treatment is directed towards stimulating these glands to produce the hormones, or, if this is not successful, the hormones can be administered exogenously.

For these treatments the following drugs are used:

127

(a) *Clomiphene (also known as Clomid)*

This is an antioestrogenic drug which seems to stimulate the production of FSH and LH by the hypothalamus and the pituitary. It is normally given for five days either at the beginning of the cycle or after menstruation has ceased. It is simple and has been successful in producing follicular growth and ovulation in a certain percentage of cases; however, it has an adverse effect on the cervical mucus which is often poor in quantity and quality. This, in turn, adversely affects sperm transport and susvival and some specialists give oestrogen during midcycle to counteract these adverse effects.

(b) *FSH and LH*

FSH is given during the follicular phase of the cycle to produce follicular growth, while Human Chorionic Gonadotrophin (HCG) is given to trigger the ovulatory event instead of LH. Occasionally, HCG is also given when Clomid is used in the cycle.

(c) Where the deficiency is in the hormones of the hypothalamus, it is possible to administer the releasing factors by continuous injections over the day. A syringe containing the hormones is worn on a belt and primed to deliver a certain amount of the releasing factors automatically every two hours, thus imitating the pulsatile release of these factors in the natural state over the cycle.

(d) *Hyperprolactaemia*

Where overproduction of prolactin is found in the circulation, a cause must be established. X-ray examination will show whether a tumour of the pituitary is present; if there is one it should be removed. Where no pituitary cause is found, the excess prolactin can be 'neutralised' by giving bromocryptine, and fertility quickly returns. Very often the woman who suffers from hyperprolactaemia may also suffer from galactorrhoea, a condition where milk leaks from the breasts on stimulation. This milk secretion also disappears on successful treatment.

All of the above treatments can be monitored by the woman using her symptothermal chart when ovulation can be easily seen if it occurs.

The luteinized unruptured follicle (LUF)
In some infertile women, an attempt at follicular growth occurs but the ovum is not released and the cycle remains anovulatory and infertile.

The underlying cause is the underproduction of oestrogen by the follicle which is insufficient to trigger the LH surge necessary for ovulation. Since a certain amount of progesterone is produced at the base of the follicle (luteinization) the condition is known as the luteinized unruptured follicle or LUF syndrome. This is a very common cause of infertility or subfertility. Cyclical bleeding usually occurs since there is some endometrial development from the oestrogen and later, when the follicle regresses, the drop in the oestrogen causes a shedding of the endometrium and a withdrawal bleed. The cycles are usually short and the bleeding scanty. Since no ovulation occurs a corpus luteum is not formed and the levels of progesterone remain low, giving rise to a monophasic temperature chart. The mucus, on the other hand, shows no cyclical pattern but is produced over the entire cycle. In other cycles the production of progesterone is sufficient to cause a temperature shift but the luteal phase high temperatures are only sustained for a few days (less than 10) before 'menstruation' begins. This is known as the Short Luteal Phase and is also associated with infertility and subfertility. It is also strongly suggestive of anovulation.

Confirmatory investigations include progesterone levels and serial follicular tracking by ultrasound to see whether ovulation occurs and, if so, to determine the size of the follicle. It is also possible with ultrasound to see no ovulation but a regression of the ovum within the ovary.

Treatment. Depending on the degree of follicular growth, several treatments may be given. Where the FSH appears to be normal it may be sufficient to give more oestrogen, supplement the ovarian production and trigger the LH surge. In other cycles it may be necessary to also give FSH and HCG. Monitoring can all be done by the symptothermal chart.

Occasionally one may find that the ovum is released but the luteal phase length still remains short. One can suppose that such an ovum can be fertilized. Many believe, however, that the progesterone is not sufficient for normal implantation and that either the blastocyst will not implant or, if it does, there could be an early miscarriage due to insufficient preparation of the endometrium and insufficient progesterone to ensure continued growth in the early weeks.

Oligoovulation
Some women ovulate both irregularly and infrequently and this may be the cause of their infertility. Such women have some dysfunction of the hypothalamic and pituitary axis with underproduction of the respective hormones. Cycles are irregular and sometimes these women are given the o/c pill to 'regularize' the cycles. This treatment is likely to depress further the hypothalamic/pituitary function and its hormones, resulting in an untreatable infertility state later, and should be refused if offered.

However, while many women with irregular cycles may appear infertile, a knowledge about fertility (fertility awareness) and the possibility of predicting high fertility in the cycle can, and often does, enable them to conceive. This understanding is also helpful in allaying anxiety and stress about fertility and future pregnancy which, in itself, is beneficial towards conceiving. A knowledge of the cervical mucus pattern is the most important indicator for women wishing to conceive; however a temperature graph is very useful over the early cycles in pinpointing anovulatory or short luteal phase cycles. Once it has been established that ovulation appears normal it is sufficient to continue with the mucus indicator.

Finally there are the 28 per cent of couples in whom no cause can be found for their infertility. These are described as ideopathic. Such couples can derive great psychological benefit from seeing a fertile chart. In addition they can seek help in choosing the optimal time in the cycle for sexual intercourse with a view to conception. Sometimes this is all such couples require to get pregnant.

2   *Uterine/cervical causes*

Tumours of the uterus may cause infertility or subfertility, especially where they encroach on the cavity of the uterus or in the cervical canal. They can be picked up by Xray (HSG, *Hysterosalpingogram*) when the contrast medium will outline the fibroid. The presence of infections in the cervix (cervicitis), or in the vagina (vaginitis) may be a cause of infertility. The infection may be acute, causing symptoms, or chronic with little or no sign of infection. More often the woman will notice a vaginal discharge which is continuous over the whole of the cycle and different from the cervical mucus.

Some of the commonest infections are Monilia (thrush), when the discharge has a cheesy white appearance, and trichamonad infection when the discharge is frothy and greenish. In other cases there is a non-specific infection and, in some cases, a viral infection of the cervix may be the cause.

Diagnosis is made by looking at the colour and type of vaginal discharge and by microscopic examination and sensitivity to antibiotics. A viral infection of the cervix is not easily treated but some clinicians use laser or cauterization in an effort to eradicate the infection.

Very often the discharge and infection go unnoticed until the woman begins to observe her mucus discharge and finds it is atypical. The NFP teacher will then be able to advise her and have further investigations performed if necessary. Fertility awareness has, therefore, an important role to play in the diagnosis of possible cervical causes of infertility.

3 Psychosexual causes

As already stated, many psychosexual problems related to infertility are a joint problem for both partners and should be jointly investigated by specialists. In some cases the psychosexual problem may itself be caused by the infertility problem and one can arrive at a vicious circle in both the diagnosis and the treatment.

A *Vaginismus*. This is a condition in the female which leads to non-consummation. It results from a spasm of the muscles surrounding the vagina which prevents the entry of the penis into the vaginal canal. On examination, no physical cause can be found for the spasm. Treatment should include the underlying psychological cause and may be helped by having the woman herself use suitable dilators for insertion into the vagina. This treatment sometimes works. Very often, women suffering from vaginismus are reluctant to discuss the problem with the doctor and may feel happier in discussing it with a sympathetic NFP teacher who should then be able to advise her on what to do.

B *Endometriosis*. This is a condition in which endometrial tissue, which normally lines the uterine cavity and is shed at menstruation, is found outside the uterus in 'ectopic' sites. The commonest place to find this ectopic endometrium is in the ovary and in the pelvic cavity around the uterus.

The cause is unknown. It does not occur before puberty and is more common in the 30 to 40 age groups. It is associated with infertility and occurs more in Caucasians than in other races.

132

The ectopic endometrial tissue bleeds internally at the time of menstruation and causes 'chocolate cysts' in the ovaries and in the pelvic cavity. Later, adhesions form and fibrosis sets in which affect the tubes and causes infertility and sometimes pelvic pain. Very often, however, the woman does not realise that she has endometriosis until she seeks investigation and treatment for infertility. Endometriosis is usually discovered at the time of laparoscopic examination.

Surgical treatment. The cysts can be removed or, if there are extensive adhesions and fibrosis, it may be necessary to remove the ovaries, tubes and uterus.

Hormonal treatment. Menstruation is suppressed for 6 to 9 months to stop the development of cysts and adhesions. The drug used for this is Danazol (Danol) which is given by mouth. At the end of 6 to 9 months Danazol is stopped and ovulation and sometimes pregnancy follow very quickly.

4 Tubal causes

In order to achieve a pregnancy, at least one healthy, patent (open) tube is required. However, the fallopian tubes are not solely passage-ways between the ovaries and the uterus, but are complex and delicate structures lined by special cells with tiny hairs attached (cilia) which help to waft the sperm from the uterus towards the outer end of the tube for fertilization and then create an opposite current to help the embryo move down the tube into the uterus for implantation.

If the tubes are completely blocked, conception is not possible as the sperm cannot get to the ovum in the outer end of the tube; if however, the tubes are damaged but not completely blocked, it is possible for conception to occur but the growing embryo is more likely to get trapped in the damaged tube, a condition known as an ectopic or tubal pregnancy. This is a dangerous situation as rupture eventually occurs causing severe bleeding which can be life-threatening.

A further problem with damaged tubes is blockage of the fimbrial end; it does not pick up the ovum when it is released from the follicle or if it does catch it, the ovum is trapped in the dense adhesions surrounding the tube. In both cases the woman is infertile.

Causes of tubal damage. The main cause of tubal blockage and damage is infection. This infection may be outside the tubes but causing adhesions of the tubes to the pelvic wall. Peritonitis and appendicitis as well as other infections in the gut can be the cause. The adhesions can be cut and removed by operation. More often an internal infection in the tubes such as gonococcus or clymidia is the cause. Such infections are acquired by sexual intercourse or as a result of using the intrauterine device for contraception, as a complication of termination of pregnancy or, more rarely today, after a miscarriage or even a fullterm delivery. A further cause today is previous sterilization.

Investigation. Tests can be carried out to find out if the tubes are blocked and there are three ways to do this.

A *Gas Insufflation (Rubin Test).* This is a very old method which is rarely used. Carbon dioxide gas is blown under pressure through the uterus and tubes. If the tubes are open the gas can be heard in the abdomen by using a stethescope over the tubal area. It has the advantage that no anaesthetic is required nor a stay in hospital.

B *Hysterosalpingogram (HSG).* In this test an Xray is taken of the uterus and tubes which are filled with a contrast medium (dye) to outline them. The radiologist can follow the passage of the contrast medium through the uterus and tubes until it spills into the abdominal cavity if the tubes are patent. If there is a blockage in the tubes or any abnormality of the uterus or tubes, the contrast medium will show it up. It also has the advantage of not requiring an anaesthetic but the disadvantage that

134

one cannot see adhesions outside the tubes which may also cause blockage.

C *Laparoscopy and hydrotubation*. This is a more complex procedure which requires an anaesthetic and usually a short stay in hospital. The abdomen is filled with carbon dioxide gas in order to see the pelvic organs more clearly. A thin tube (laparoscope) is inserted into the abdomen close to the umbilicus and a small telescope is inserted through the tube. Through this the examiner can clearly see the uterus, tubes and ovaries. The presence of adhesions can be noted. An assistant then injects a blue dye through the cervix and it passes through the uterus and tubes spilling out into the abdominal cavity if the tubes are patent. If there is a blockage in the tubes the examiner can note the site. This is useful information for later surgery on the tubes.

Tubal surgery treatment

Tubal transplantation has been tried but, so far, without success. Surgical intervention aims at unblocking the tubes or releasing the adhesions in the pelvis when these are present. Where the adhesions are in the pelvis outside the tubes they can be cut without causing much trauma and since the lining of the tubes is not damaged, this operation usually achieves a high success rate. Where the tubal lining is damaged, operations to undo the blockage, despite newer surgical techniques such as using a specially designed microscope or laser to aid surgery, does not enjoy a similar happy result. Even in centres of excellence one cannot expect more than a 30 per cent success rate.

New reproductive technologies

Despite the advances in treatment for infertility, by the 1970s less than 50 per cent of infertile couples managed to achieve a pregnancy. The development of a technique whereby the ovum could be fertilized outside the body and the resulting embryo transferred back to the uterus hit the headlines in 1977 when Steptoe and Edwards, from Loughborough and Cambridge respectively, reported the first successful human pregnancy using this method. Since then this technique has become available in almost every country in the world and, by 1988, has resulted in over 5,000 births.

Invitro fertilization (IVF)
Sometimes known incorrectly as 'test-tube babies' the term means fertilization in glass. The fertilization is not accomplished in a test-tube but in a flat, glass dish known as a Petrie dish. The egg is taken from the ovary and fertilized with sperm obtained from the partner by masturbation. The resulting embryo is then transferred back to the uterus approximately 50 hours after its original collection from the ovary, or two days after fertilization.

Usually ovulation is induced by drugs and the growth of the follicle is followed with hormone assays and ultrasound measurements. When the ovum is judged to be mature it is removed by one of several techniques, transferred into the Petrie dish and fertilized.

Normally several follicles are developed and several eggs are retrieved. This is done for two reasons: a) it has been found by experience that the likelihood of a successful pregnancy is increased when more than one embryo is transferred, and b) 'spare embryos' can be frozen and used for transfer at a later time if no successful implantation has occurred, or if the woman wishes a further pregnancy in the future.

Methods for ovum retrieval. Laparoscopy was originally used to recover the ovum, and is still used in some centres. It has the disadvantage that a general anaesthetic is required, and where there are dense adhesions around the tubes and ovaries it is not always possible to get the needle correctly positioned to puncture the follicle and recover the egg.

Transvesicle ovum retrieval. This is done under local anaesthetic. The suction probe is guided by ultrasound through the bladder, the follicle is punctured and the ovum recovered in the syringe. This has a further advantage in that the probe can be guided through adhesions which do not cause problems. Damage to the bladder is minimal in practice.

Transvaginal ovum retrieval. Using this route, the suction probe is guided by ultrasound through the vagina instead of the bladder. Local anaesthetic is used and the patient can return home in the interval between ovum retrieval and embryo transfer.

The indications for IVF are mainly tubal damage where surgery has not been successful. However, cases where males are afflicted with oligospermia; where the cervical mucus has been found hostile to sperms and where couples suffer from unexplained infertility have all been treated with some success. The success rate is, however, very low. The best figures claim about 20 per cent success rate which is less than the success rate for tubal surgery. IVF involves a large team of workers and is costly in both time and money. It is even more costly psychologically for the 70–80 per cent of couples for whom it is unsuccessful despite repeated treatments.

Gamete Intrafallopian Transfer (GIFT)

This is a variety of assisted reproduction which does not involve invitro fertilization. Using this method the ovum and sperm are transferred into the fallopian tube where fertilization, if it occurs, will take place. It presupposes that at least one of the tubes is healthy and open. The semen specimen for fertilization which is inserted into the tube is obtained by masturbation and this technique is not acceptable to some cultures and religions.

Low tubal ovum transfer (LTOT)
When the tubes are blocked or diseased, the ovum can be transferred into the uterus; fertilization is then effected by normal intercourse or by artificial insemination. The success rate of this technique is less than that of GIFT but of course these couples would not be eligible for GIFT because of tubal damage. The success rate may also be less than that for IVF but on the other hand it is culturally and ethically acceptable to certain groups for whom IVF is not acceptable.

Tubal ovum transfer (TOT)
This is a further variation of GIFT in which one or more ova are transferred transvaginally from the ovary to the outer end of the tube under ultrasound guidance, using a local anaesthetic. This requires at least one tube to be open as with GIFT: The woman is then allowed home to have normal intercourse. Results vary but many couples have achieved a pregnancy in this way and it is acceptable ethically and culturally where GIFT is not.

Complications encountered with assisted reproductive techniques
The low success rate is the biggest problem. This is further aggravated by the following:

(a) Ectopic pregnancies occur in about 5 per cent of those who become pregnant.
(b) Multiple pregnancies occur much more often than normal. A report from Australia states that twins occurred in 30 per cent and triplets in 33 per cent of their 'successful' pregnancies. These multiple pregnancies are further complicated by small and premature babies with a higher-than-usual perinatal mortality. The Australian study reported an incidence of 27 per cent preterm babies and 33 per cent low-birthweight babies in the series.
(c) Spontaneous miscarriage in those embryos who

138

implant successfully occurs in approximately 30 per cent of cases.

(d) Despite detailed and fastidious selection of 'healthy' sperm to fertilize the ova, the incidence of congenital abnormalities including that of Down's syndrome was 2.6 per cent in the Australian report. The normal incidence of congenital abnormalities in Australia was only 1.6 per cent.

(e) To some couples it is ethically unacceptable.

All of these complications add to the psychological trauma of the couple. Careful counselling should be sought before embarking on the treatment and not after, as often happens in practice.

Conclusion
Despite brilliant advances in the treatment of infertility, there is a lot about fertilization and implantation still unknown and there are an appreciable number of couples who will remain childless.

A major step for such couples is the acceptance and acknowledgement of this infertility in such a manner that it does not lead to lifelong bitterness and regret. NFP teachers and clinics can have a vital role in helping couples to come to terms in a constructive manner with this.

See also guidelines for referral to specialist clinics.

9

The new technologies

The two main problems for couples using natural family planning methods are the daily chore of observation and charting and the subjective assessment of her fertility by the woman. There have recently been rapid developments in technologies to detect the fertile phase in the cycle. So far these have been developed for the investigation of infertility, but they can be used with limitations to make the process of natural family planning simpler and more objective. However, with further developments there is the possibility that within years individual couples, in their own home environments, will be able to detect precisely the beginning and the end of the fertile phase. This would increase the accessibility, and therefore the acceptability, of natural family planning.

There is a very aggressive and competitive marketing campaign for a whole range of recently developed products, many of which are now available over the counter in pharmacies throughout the country. It is important to be aware of the advantages and disadvantages before buying these comparatively expensive packages.

Over the past 5 years products have come and gone; many have been tried and tested as aids to NFP methods but have been found wanting. I shall list the tests that have 'survived' and/or improved and which I believe might be useful to NFP programmes and users.

140

Urinary dipsticks/pads and colour changes

The Luteinizing (LH) Dipstick
The LH dipstick has been available for several years but had the disadvantage that home-kits required fairly complex techniques and took a considerable amount of time to carry out.

After several years of experimentation, a one-step LH dipstick which can be carried out in a matter of seconds and gives a result in a few minutes has finally arrived on the market. This test is known as the Clearplan one-step LH test. The dipstick is held in the stream of the first urine in the morning and the results are immediately available. Depending on the cycle length, the test is carried out for 5 days (normal and short cycles) or 10 days (long cycles). This test is particularly useful for women or couples who wish to detect high fertility in the cycle in order to conceive. For couples wishing to avoid or postpone a pregnancy, it does not give sufficient advance warning of ovulation for this purpose.

Test kits for oestrodiol and pregnanediol in urine
For NFP users who wish to limit or postpone their families, test kits for the urinary detection of the metabolites of oestrogen and progesterone are required. These enable the limits of the fertile phase to be more easily defined.

The development of simple urinary assays for the oestrogen metabolites to detect the beginning of the fertile phase has proved more difficult than anticipated, and to date there is no simple urinary test available to demarcate the first fertile day.

In contrast, the Progesturine TM PDG assay now available is a monoclonal antibody-base, competitive, colorimetric, enzyme immunoassay (EIA) for the qualitative detection of Pregnanediol glucoronide (PDG), the metabolite of progesterone found in the urine. This test can be used to demarcate the end of the fertile phase. The test is performed on a rapid absorbent matrix pad (RAMP), and a PDG colour reference is used for comparison.

141

A single drop of undiluted urine is placed on the matrix pad to which later is added an enzyme conjugate and a substrate solution. The final result will be no colour change (indicating high pregnanediol levels) or a dark blue spot which is equal to or darker than the reference colour (indicating low pregnanediol levels). The test only takes 5 minutes to perform and the results are immediately available.

The manufacturers recommend that the test be performed on 3 consecutive days during the mid-luteal phase of the cycle and the LH dipstick surge day is recommended as a reference for testing.

NFP users, who use the peak mucus day as the reference day for ovulation, found the test indicated luteal levels of pregnanediol on the 4th day after the peak mucus day in a high percentage of cycles.

However, the test is neither suitably packaged nor as yet simple enough for use as a home-kit. It comes in a package of 50 tests with a shelf life of a year which is clearly too many for one individual woman. Furthermore, although the test only takes 5 minutes it is as yet too complicated for an unskilled person to do at home.

We believe that this test shows great promise and could be developed within a short time to become available to NFP users. It could prove to be a substitute for the BBT either completely or in cycles, where the BBT is unreliable to interpret because of disturbances, or as a double-check with cervical mucus to confirm the end of the fertile days in the cycle.

Measurement of changes in body fluids
There are changes in the amount of vaginal fluid (transudate) during the cycle under the influence of oestrogen and progesterone. Vaginal transudate is increased in the high oestrogen phase and decreased in the progesterone phase in a similar manner to mucus volumes. The development of a small, plastic, graduated, disposable vaginal aspirator, the Rovumeter, makes it possible to spirate the combined mucus and vaginal fluid (cervico-

142

vaginal fluid – CVF) and accurately measures the amount aspirated. There is a tenfold increase in cervico-vaginal fluid volume in the fertile phase of the cycle, with a sharp drop to almost non-existent levels after ovulation. In practice, the aspiration has only to be done over 10 days of the cycle to detect these changes. Studies have shown that this technique can be used with a minimum of instruction and with no complications. It is very acceptable to women especially in the learning stages of the cervical mucus method when there is often some doubt and confusion about the quality of the mucus present or at a later stage when the mucus symptom is not distinct and clear. At the moment the Rovumeter is a valuable adjunct for users of the cervical mucus method. Further refinements are required before it can be used exclusively to avoid pregnancy.

Measurement of changes in electrical resistance
The electrical resistance of the vagina, saliva and skin change during the menstrual cycle due to the changing levels of sex hormones and techniques have been developed to measure these changes with a view to detecting the fertile phase of the cycle. These methods are not as yet widely used and almost not at all in this country. The Cue Fertility Monitor, which measures and compares the electrical resistance of the vagina and of saliva, has been produced by ZETEX, Aurora, Colorado, USA, and is being researched in the United States and West Germany.

Digital and electronic thermometers
Technological advances in the development of thermometers have had beneficial repercussions for those women who use the BBT method of natural family planning. Digital thermometers are now in common use in hospitals and clinics, and are also being used for NFP. They have the advantage of reducing the recording time from five minutes (clinical thermometer) to 45 seconds. The digital read-out facilitates easy and reliable reading, and a

microprocessor calculates the rate of change of temperature and gives an audible 'beep' when the temperature reaches equilibrium. Many women who have had erratic charts with the clinical thermometer have found that their records became interpretable when using a digital thermometer. They are battery-operated and usually have a battery life of 3 years. Some have a memory which stores the temperature until the next reading (Phillips with memory).

Two electronic thermometers are on the market. The first Rite-time rhythm clock combines an electronic thermometer and a battery-operated calculator. A temperature probe is used to measure the BBT and the reading is displayed on a small screen. The daily BBT measurements are stored in the computer which can indicate to the woman that the post-ovulatory phase has begun. Clinical trials in England have shown the Rite-time to be both accurate and reliable, but it has the disadvantage that no temperature chart is available for assessment or retrospective analysis. An advantage is that the device can be programmed to adjust for changes in the BBT related to the circadian rhythm; marketing has been poor for this product and it is becoming increasingly difficult to buy it in the UK.

The second electronic thermometer is the Bioself 110 Fertility Indicator, a more intricate and sophisticated version of an electronic thermometer. In this device, the thermometer works in a similar manner to the Rite-time except that no temperature reading is displayed. The device uses a combination of the calendar and temperature methods to detect the fertile and infertile phases of the cycle, and indicates by means of signal lights the fertility level for any particular day in the cycle. Green light indicates fertility; a steady red light indicates possible low fertility and a flashing red light denotes high fertility.

By plugging the thermometer probe into a printer at the end of the cycle, it is possible to obtain the temperature graph for the cycle. Early studies have shown the technical ability of the analyzer to demarcate the fertile days in the cycle and we have just completed a survey of the efficiency of the Bioself for use in couples wishing to avoid or postpone a pregnancy. One hundred and twenty women used the Bioself Fertility Indicator, for a minimum of one year, as the sole method to determine the fertile phase in order to postpone or avoid a pregnancy. Among the group, there was only one unplanned pregnancy resulting from a failure of the Bioself. There was high acceptability for the device among the users, many of whom continued to use it after the study period. We are presently testing out a new, updated version of the device, the Bioself 120. This latest model displays the actual temperature reading in addition to the signal lights and it can be plugged into the telephone system at the end of the cycle to obtain a printout of the BBT graph.

The Bioself 110 is presently available in Switzerland and Canada; the latest Bioself 120 will be on the market in the UK at the end of 1990.

Computers

Most natural family planning programmes have access to large computers in statistical departments of medical and research centres for analyses of data (mainly charts) collected by the programmes. Computers save time and labour and allow many cross-correlations of data to be made with ease and speed. Consequently, more recent natural family planning graphs and charts are being designed for such computer interpretation.

Small battery-operated personal computers are now available into which clinical data can be entered and degrees of fertility obtained. One such is called the Ovia, a home computer. This correlates temperature, mucus patterns and cervical changes to indicate varying degrees of fertility. The results are displayed on a small screen which can sit on a bedside locker or be carried in a handbag.

Using the new technologies

Natural family planning programmes address a couple in its totality as two human beings, and the behavioural component of sexuality cannot be solved, although at times it may be helped, by technology. But technology can fail or err, and in such circumstances, it is the basic knowledge of fertility and sexuality which can come to the rescue. If a couple is to be successful in creating a happy and responsible family life, such basic knowledge has to be acquired and developed irrespective of present or future technological developments and aids.

Since a correct knowledge and use of the signs of fertility (temperature, cervical mucus patterns and other clinical symptoms) offers a highly efficient method of birth regulation independent of drugs or devices, many couples question whether the introduction of technology into natural family planning programmes is detracting from the 'naturalness' of the methods. The instruments and devices used in the new technologies do not necessarily interfere with sexuality and its expression, but on the contrary, may even help to deepen our understanding of the refined natural mechanisms which operate in reproduction and fertility, and increase our admiration and respect for the natural. Through the judicious use of technology couples may find themselves better prepared to take an increased and shared responsibility for their relationships and for planning their families.

10

Questions and answers

Q I have been prescribed a course of antibiotics by my
   doctor for an infection. Is it likely that these drugs will
   interfere with the mucus method that we use?
A Some drugs do affect the menstrual cycle and cause
   problems with the observation and interpretation of
   the fertility indicators. Occasionally, women taking
   antibiotics have reported a change in their normal
   cervical mucus pattern. However, it is difficult to assess whether the antibiotics themselves or the stress
   caused by the illness for which the drugs were prescribed are responsible for these changes in the mucus
   secretions.

   Certainly, if you are taking drugs you should be
   aware of the possibility of these affecting the menstrual
   cycle in some way. Continuing to chart as usual
   will soon demonstrate any irregularities as a consequence of the drugs, in which case it is wise to
   'double-check' by charting two or more of the fertility signs to help in the interpretation of each indicator.

   Drugs that can cause irregularities in the menstrual
   cycle include:

1 Several tranquillisers (such as Stelazine or Haloperi-
   dol); drugs used to treat migraine, nausea and vom-
   iting (such as Maxolon); and some drugs used for
   travel sickness. These latter produce increased levels

of prolactin in the bloodstream and so are liable to delay or even suppress ovulation.

2   Preparations of oestrogen and progesterone. These are sometimes used in the treatment of gynaecological disorders and affect both the quality and quantity of cervical mucus. Also, the hormones can be stored in the fatty tissue of the body and released slowly over a long period, so their effects may be felt for some time after the drugs have been discontinued. (This occasionally happens when women stop taking the oral contraceptive pill.)

3   Cortisone. These preparations are commonly used for allergies such as hay fever, asthma and rheumatic problems. As there is a close link between the adrenal hormones (cortisone) and the ovarian hormones, the use of cortisone, particularly over long periods, may well cause irregularities in the menstrual cycle.

4   Antihistamine drugs. These are prescribed to dry up excessive mucous membrane secretions. As the cervix is a mucous membrane, there is always the risk that the drying effect will also disrupt secretions of cervical mucus.

5   Drugs used in the treatment of cancer.

If you are prescribed drugs, particularly on a long-term basis, it is advisable to talk to your NFP counsellor about any possible side-effects related to the menstrual cycle and the best ways of tackling these.

Q   Is there an increased risk of having an abnormal baby if you use natural family planning methods?

A   The question of the relationship between congenital abnormalities as a consequence of aging sperm or an over-ripe ovum and natural family planning methods rears its head periodically in journals and books, causing understandable apprehension among users of the methods. The first point to make, therefore, is that all the scientific evidence to date gives no reason to suspect that modern natural family planning methods lead to an increased risk of congenital abnormalities.

In the first place all the experiments that led to this suspicion were conducted on animals and involved the deliberate aging of sperm and ova prior to fertilisation. There are, however, several differences between results obtained in such experimental conditions on animals and those occurring under normal and natural circumstances in a human couple, which may well invalidate making extrapolations from one to the other.

Although not much is known about the life cycle of the sperm, particularly once it is in the woman's reproductive system, it is known that the woman's cervical mucus is designed as a remarkable filtering mechanism to 'weed out' any abnormal or damaged sperm, thus reducing the risk of an unhealthy sperm being successful in reaching the ovum. Also, estimates of the age of the ovum, which has a lifespan of only 10–12 hours, must be viewed with scepticism. As a result the suggestion that congenital abnormalities can be attributed to the fertilisation of an over-ripe ovum in a normal fertile woman is also open to question.

A study conducted by the World Health Organisation looked at couples using the ovulation method who became pregnant at the extreme limits of the fertile phase (when there is the greatest chance of an overmature ovum or sperm). It was found that there was no increased incidence of congenital abnormalities among these babies.

Certainly, the time is ripe for further, more searching investigations into this question, but in the meantime couples practising natural methods or thinking about doing so can rest assured that there is no medical evidence to support the suggestion of a link between such methods and an increased risk of an abnormal baby.

Q I read that natural methods can be used to influence the sex of a baby. Is this correct?

A Whether or not it is possible to influence the sex of a baby is a highly controversial point. It is certainly one that has fascinated people for centuries; Aristotle's answer was to advise those couples who wanted to conceive a boy to have sexual intercourse in the north wind. Couples who wanted a girl, on the other hand, were instructed to have intercourse in the south wind!

Research is still being carried out today to try to crack the problem. An American gynaecologist, Dr L. Shettles, puts forward the theory that it is the timing of sexual intercourse that is the crucial factor in determining the sex of a baby. He based this on his discovery that sperm carrying the female chromosome had a greater capacity for surviving in a slightly acidic environment than sperm carrying the male chromosome. He also found that sperm carrying the male chromosome travelled through the woman's reproductive system much faster than sperm carrying the female chromosome.

This led him to propose the following: couples who want a boy should abstain from sexual intercourse until as close as possible to the time of ovulation; the woman's cervical mucus is at its most fertile at this time and therefore both thinner in consistency and more alkaline to assist the rapid movement of the sperm carrying the male chromosome and favour its survival.

Couples who desire a girl should, in contrast, have intercourse two or three days before ovulation when the mucus is slightly more acidic, which is advantageous to sperm carrying the female chromosome.

However the results of a study obtained by Professor J. France of the University of Auckland, New Zealand, clearly refute the theory that intercourse close to ovulation favours male conception. Further studies are required in this field before we can arrive at any conclusion.

Glossary

Abstinence	See *Periodic Abstinence*
Amenorrhoea	Prolonged absence of a menstrual period.
Anovulatory Menstrual cycle	A menstrual cycle in which ovulation does not occur.
Basal Body Temperature	The temperature of the body at rest, normally taken immediately after awakening in the morning and before rising.
Basal Body Temperature of NFP	A natural method of family planning in which the postovulatory infertile phase of the menstrual cycle is identified by a sustained temperature rise.
Birth Control	See *Family Planning*
Bladder	A muscular sac which stores urine before it is discharged through the urethra.
Breast feeding	The physiological process by which the baby receives its nourishment directly from the breasts. The amount may be total (ecological; on demand; unrestricted) or partial.
Calendar Method	A method of family planning in which the fertile time in the menstrual cycle is calculated from the duration of previous menstrual cycles. Also called *rhythm method*.
Cervical Crypts	Pockets of cells in the lining of the cervix which secrete mucus.
Cervical Mucus	The fluid produced by the cells lining the cervix. The quantity and quality of the mucus are influenced by the sex hormones.
Cervical Mucus	INFERTILE-TYPE has a sticky appearance and denotes low levels of oestrogen.
	FERTILE-TYPE is stretchy, lubricative, slippery mucus which normally occurs close to ovulation.
Cervical Mucus Method of NFP	A method of family planning by which a woman assesses the changes in the quality of mucus as a means of identifying the fertile and infertile phases of the menstrual cycle.

151

Cervical os	The opening of the lower end of the uterus which can be felt through the vagina.
Climacteric	The phase in a woman's life when reproductive function is declining (see also *Premenopause*).
Clitoris	A small erectile body which responds to sexual stimulation and is situated anteriorly between the labia.
Coitus	The word is used synonymously with SEXUAL INTERCOURSE.
	COITUS INTERRUPTUS ⎱ See *Intercourse,*
	COITUS RESERVATUS ⎰ *Sexual*
Contraception	See *Family Planning*
Corpus Luteum (Yellow body)	An endocrine gland that develops from the empty sac left in the ovary after ovulation. It secretes the hormones progesterone in increased quantitiesuntil the end of the cycle and shrivels up if a pregnancy does not occur.
Cover Line	A technique for interpreting a shift in the basal body temperature graph.
Ectopic Gestation	The implantation of a fertilised ovum outside the uterus, usually in the fallopian tube.
Ejaculation	The emission of semen from the penis during male orgasm.
Embryo	An unborn child in the very earliest stages of development. Often also referred to as a fetus.
Endocrine Gland	A gland without ducts that produces and releases hormones directly into the bloodstream.
Endometrium	The inner lining of the uterus which is shed during menstruation. In pregnancy the fertilised egg implants in the endometrium.
Erection	The enlargement and hardening of the penis which makes penetration into the vagina possible.
Fallopian Tube	The two tubes which extend from the upper part of the uterus to the ovaries. Through these tubes the ova pass from the ovaries to the uterus and sperm pass from the uterus towards the ovaries. Fertilisation takes place in the outer end of the tubes.
Family Planning	This term is usually interchangeable with BIRTH CONTROL. It means the conscious use by sexually active couples of methods to achieve, space or avoid pregnancies. Natural family planning methods can be used to achieve or avoid pregnancy; other methods can only be used to prevent pregnancy (contraception).

Glossary

Fertile Phase The days of the menstrual cycle during which sexual intercourse or genital contact can result in a pregnancy.

Fertilisation The union of the sperm and the ovum. It normally occurs in the outer end of the fallopian tube.

Gamete The mature male or female reproductive cell, the sperm and ovum.

Graafian Follicle A small fluid-filled cavity in the ovary which contains the ovum.

Genital Contact Contact of the penis with the vulva without penetration.

GIFT A method of assisted reproduction. The ovum and sperm are placed into the fallopian tube where fertilization takes place. It presupposes that at least one tube is healthy and open.

Hormone A chemical substance produced and secreted by an endocrine gland (i.e. the corpus luteum). Hormones are carried by the blood to produce a response in an organ, known as a *target organ*, sensitive to that hormone. *Oestrogen* is a hormone that stimulates the development and function of the woman's reproductive system and the fertile-type mucus. *Progesterone* is a hormone that prepares the reproductive system for a possible pregnancy. *Testosterone* is a hormone produced by the testes that stimulates the development and function of the man's reproductive system.

Implanation The process by which the fertilised ovum embeds in the endometrium.

Intercourse, Sexual COMPLETE. Sexual activity during which the penis is inserted into the vagina where ejaculation takes place.

INCOMPLETE COITUS INTERRUPTUS or withdrawal. Here the penis is deliberately withdrawn from the vagina before ejaculation. Ejaculation occurs outside the vagina.

COITUS RESERVATUS. Sexual activity in which the penis is inserted into the vagina but ejaculation is deliberately avoided.

Intermenstrual Bleeding Bleeding occurring between two menstruations usually round the time of ovulation and sometimes called *ovulatory bleeding*.

Intermenstrual Pain Sometimes called MITTELSCHMERZ. Abdominal pain occurring in the right or left lower abdomen between two menstruations and closely related to ovulation.

153

IVF	A method of assisted reproduction. The ovum and sperm are placed in a glass dish where fertilization takes place. The resulting embryo is later transferred to the uterine cavity for implantation.
Labia	The two sets of lips surrounding the entrance to the vagina.
Lactation	The production of milk by the breasts.
Leucorrhoea	An abnormal discharge from the vagina. The colour varies depending on whether or not infection is present.
Menarche	The first menstrual period a woman experiences.
Menopause	The last menstrual period a woman experiences at the end of her reproductive life. A woman who has not menstruated for one year is described as being postmenopausal.
Menstrual Cycle	The cyclic occurrence of a series of physiological changes in ovaries, the endometrium and the cervix.
Menstrual Cycle, Length of	The number of days from the first day of menstrual bleeding to the day before the following menstruation.
Menstrual Cycle, Phases of	For NFP purposes, there are three phases in the cycle: 1 The preovulatory, relatively infertile phase. 2 The periovulatory fertile phase. 3 The postovulatory, absolutely infertile phase.
Menstruation (Menses, Period)	The cyclic shedding of the endometrium, consisting of blood, mucus and dead cells.
Metabolism	A process of life by which dead tissue cells are destroyed and renewed.
Mittelschmerz	See *Intermenstrual Pain*
Mucorrhoea	Normal flow of mucus from the vagina.
Mucus	See *Cervical Mucus*
Multiparous Woman	A woman who has had one or more babies.
Multiple-index Methods of NFP	NFP methods where a combination of several clinical indicators of fertility are used to detect the fertile time in the cycle.
Natural Family Planning	Methods for planning or avoiding pregnancies by observation of the naturally occurring signs and symptoms of the fertile and infertile phase of the menstrual cycle. It is implicit in the definition of natural family planning, when used to avoid conception, that drugs, devices and surgical procedures are not used, there is abstinence from sexual intercourse during the fertile phase of the

menstrual cycle and the act of intercourse, when it occurs, is complete.

Nulliparous Woman   A woman who has never given birth to a child.

Oestrogen   See *Hormone*

Orgasm   The climax of sexual excitement and pleasure in the man or the woman. In the man it is accompanied by ejaculation.

Ovaries   The sex glands of the woman which produce ova and hormones that control female reproduction and female secondary sexual characteristics.

Ovulation   The release of a mature egg from the ovarian (Graafian) follicle.

Ovum   The mature female reproductive germ cell, or egg. (Plural: ova.)

Periodic Abstinence   Voluntary avoidance, by a couple, of sexual intercourse during the fertile phase of the cycle in order to avoid a pregnancy.

Pre-ejaculatory Fluid   A small amount of fluid discharged involuntarily from the penis during sexual excitement. It may contain viable sperm.

Premenopause   The months or years preceding the menopause when some irregularities in the menstrual cycle may occur.

Primipara   A woman giving birth to her first child.

Progesterone   See *Hormone*

Prostate   A gland in the man's reproductive system, situated at the base of the bladder and surrounding the upper part of the urethra. Its secretions form part of the seminal fluid.

Puberty   The time during which the reproductive organs become functional and the secondary sexual characteristics appear.

Scrotum   The bag of skin which contains the testes.

Semen   The fluid ejaculated from the penis containing sperm cells and secretions from the prostate and seminal vesicles.

Seminal vesicle (sperm sacs)   Two sacs lying near the top of the prostate gland. They contribute fluid to help form the semen.

Single-index Methods of NFP   Methods of natural family planning where only one clinical indicator is used to detect the fertile phase in the cycle.

Sperm   The mature male reproductive germ cell(s).

Spotting   Small amounts of red or brown discharge which occur during the menstrual cycle outside the time of menstrual flow.

Symptothermal Methods of NFP	A method of family planning in which the pre and postovulatory infertile phases of the menstrual cycle are identified by changes in the basal body temperature, changes in the cervix and cervical mucus. Other signs and symptoms may also be used, e.g. breast changes, intermenstrual pain and/or bleeding. Calendar calculations may be used to help estimate the end of the preovulatory relatively infertile phase.
Testes	The man's sex glands which produce sperm and hormones that contribute to the male secondary sex characteristics.
Testosterone	See *Hormone*
Unplanned Pregnancy	A pregnancy that the couple did not intend and which occurred despite the use of a family planning method to avoid a pregnancy.
Urethra	A narrow tube extending in women from the bladder to the vulva and in men traversing the penis and opening at its end. In men and women the urethra conveys urine from the bladder to the exterior of the body. In men it also conveys the semen.
Uterus	A hollow muscular organ in which the fertilised ovum implants and grows. It is usually called the womb.
Vagina	A hollow muscular passage extending from the vulva to the cervix.
Vaginal Discharge	Fluid or other material coming from the vagina which may be normal or abnormal (menstrual bleeding is not called vaginal discharge).
Vas Deferens (Sperm Duct)	A narrow tube through which sperm are transported from the testes. (Plural: vasa deferentia.)
Vulva	The external genital organs of the woman which include the labia majora (large or outer lips), the labia minora (small or inner lips), and the clitoris.

Appendix 1   Useful addresses

Area co-ordinators of the National Association of Natural Family Planning Teachers. They will be able to give you information about local NFP clinics and teachers.

BEDFORDSHIRE
Kenneth H. Kavanagh
5 Byron Crescent
Bedford MK40 2BD

BIRMINGHAM
NFP Centre
Birmingham Maternity Hospital
Queen Elizabeth Medical Centre
Birmingham B15 2TG
Tel: 021 472 1377 Ext. 4219

BRISTOL
NFP Centre
Room 8
Central Health Clinic
Tower Hill
Bristol BS2 0JD
Tel: 0272 291010 Ext. 223

CAMBRIDGESHlRE
Mrs Elizabeth Hoey
7 Bedford Row
Foul Anchor
Tydd
Wisbech
Cambridgeshire PE13 5RF

CORNWALL AND DEVON
Dr and Mrs R. Paisey
White Hill House
18 White Hill Road
Highweek
Newton Abbot TQ12 6PR
Tel: 0626 54758 evenings

COVENTRY
Mrs G. Haverty
73 The Chesils
Coventry CV3 5BE

CUMBRIA
Mrs C. Bowman
Old Post Office
Kirkcambeck
Brampton
Cumbria

GLOUCESTERSHIRE
Mrs E. Brooke
4 St. Michael's Road
The Woodlands
Cheltenham GL51 5RR
Tel: 0242 521766

HAMPSHIRE
Mrs M. Bird
7 Chawton Park Road
Alton
Hampshire GU34 1RG

HEREFORD AND WORCESTER
Mrs Monica Russell
The Old School House
Church Road
Clehonger
Hereford HR22 9SP
Tel: 0432 277510

LANCASHIRE/MANCHESTER
Mrs M.T. Robinson, SRN, HV
1 Lawnswood
Castleton
Rochdale
Lancashire OL11 3HB

Mrs S.M. Wright, SRN, SCM
24 Leomington Road
Lytham St. Anne's
Lancashire FY8 1UA

LEICESTERSHIRE
Mrs A. James, SRN
Family Planning Clinic
St. Peter's Health Centre
Leicester
Tel: 0533 625162

Mrs J. Kennedy
46 Town Green Street
Rothley
Leicestershire LE7 7NU
Tel: 0533 302061

LIVERPOOL
Mrs W. Worthington, SRN,
   RFN, SCM
28 Dooley Drive
Old Roan
Merseyside L30 8RS
Tel: 051 526 7663

LONDON
Mrs E. Gregory
4 Heath Villas
Plumstead
London SE18 1PG
Tel: 081 855 2013

LONDON
The Catholic Marriage
   Advisory Council (CMAC)
Clitherow House
1 Blythe Mews
Blythe Road
London W14 0NW
Tel: 071 371 1341

LONDON/SURREY
Mrs R.D.M. Byrne, SRN, HV
51 Ditton Road
Surbiton
Surrey KT6 6RF
Tel: 081 399 4789

MIDDLESEX
Dr V. Zammit
10 Shepherds Close
Manor Farm Road
Shepperton
Middlesex

NORTH EAST
Miss J. Wood
'Pittsgate', Pondicherry Road
Rothsbury
Northumberland NE65 7YN
Tel: 0669 20236

NORTH WEST (*see* LIVERPOOL)

NOTTINGHAM
Mrs Clare Orger
10 Buckingham Road
Woodthorpe
Nottingham NG5 4GE
Tel: 0602 262684

SCOTLAND
Mrs Teresa McManus
c/o Archdiocesan Offices
196 Clyde Street
Glasgow G1 4JY
Tel: 041 221 0858

SHEFFIELD
Mrs J. Perryman
143 Greenhill Main Road
Sheffield S8 7RH
Tel: 0742 373301

SHROPSHIRE
Mrs P. Bailes, SRN
97 Burnmeadow Road
Newport
Shropshire TF10 7NX
Tel: 0952 812810

STAFFORDSHIRE
Mrs J. Woodward, SRN
Stafford Central Clinic
North Walls
Staffordshire
Tel: 0785 223099

SURREY (*see* LONDON)

SWINDON
Mr and Mrs R. Stroud
28 Nythe Road
Stratton St. Margaret
Swindon, Wilts, SN3 4AN
Tel: 0793 825980

TYNE AND WEAR
Mrs S. Manley
2 Moorfield
High West Jesmond
Newcastle upon Tyne NE2 5NL

NORTH WALES
Sr. Eileen
Oteley House
Salisbury Road
Wrexham,
Clwydd, LI13 7AS

Mrs W.P. Haynes
10 Oaklands Crescent
Tattenhall
Chester
Tel: 0829 70697

SOUTH WALES
Mrs. C Norman
218 Heathwood Road
Heath
Cardiff, CF4 4BS
Tel: 0222 754628

IRELAND
The Association of Natural
    Family Planning Teachers
    of Ireland
131 Worehampton Road
Donnybrook
Dublin 4
Tel: 01 693203

Appendix 2 Further reading

General

My Body, My Health: The Concerned Woman's Book of Gynaecology.
Felicia Stewart, Gary Stewart and Robert Hatcher. Chichester: John
Wiley, 1979.

The Good Health Guide for Women. Dr Cynthia W. Cooke and Susan
Dworkin. London: Hamlyn, 1981.

The New Woman's Health Handbook. Nancy McKeith (ed.). London:
Virago, 1978.

Our Bodies, Ourselves. Angela Phillips and Jill Rakusen. Harmondsworth: Penguin, 1979.

From Woman to Woman. Lucienne Lanson. Harmondsworth: Penguin,
1980.

Natural Family Planning

The Art of Natural Family Planning. John and Sheila Kippley. Cincinnati:
Couple to Couple League, 1975.

The Billings Method. Dr Evelyn Billings and Ann Westmore. Harmondsworth: Penguin, 1980.

Fertility: A Comprehensive Guide to Natural Family Planning. Dr E. Clubb
and Jane Knight. London: David & Charles, 1987.

The Natural Family Plan. Dr Anna M. Flynn and Amanuensis Books
Limited. Leicester: Windward, 1989.

Natural Family Planning. World Health Organization, Geneva, 1988.

Natural Fertility Awareness. John and Farida Davidson. Saffron Walden:
C. W. Daniels Co Ltd, 1986.

Natural Birth Control: a practical guide to fertility awareness. Kacia and
Jonathan Drake. Northampton: Thorson, 1984.

Natural Sex. Mary Shivanandan. London: Hamlyn, 1979.

An extensive reading list of material published on Natural Family Planning can be obtained from the NFP Centre, Queen Elizabeth Medical
Centre, Edgbaston, Birmingham B15 2TG.

APPENDIX 3   Recommendations for NFP teachers on client referral

A vital role of the natural family planning instructor is to assess the client who is attempting to achieve a pregnancy, and to provide referral to a gynaecologist or fertility specialist when appropriate. Though it is not within the realm of the instructor to diagnosis a potential fertility problem, the instructor does have an adequate knowledge base about fertility to be alert to the signs of a possible problem.

The following recommendations for referral should be discussed with the medical director and others who are responsible for establishing medical protocols for the agency or programme.

Recommendations for Referral:

1 During the first cycle of charting the male partner can be investigated by way of a sperm count or a post-coital test. The couples' GP can be of help here.

2 Refer a couple to a physician if, by the end of the sixth cycle of charting and timing intercourse properly, a pregnancy has not resulted. Though some physicians will not begin a fertility evaluation until the couple has attempted to conceive for one year, other physicians will initiate an evaluation if he/she knows that the couple has been following natural family planning for six menstrual cycles, particularly if the couple is thirty years or older.

3 A woman should be referred to a physician if *three* consecutive cycles of correct observation and recording of fertility signs have revealed:

   (a) a luteal phase of ten days or less from the day of the thermal shift to bleeding;
   (b) a luteal phase of ten days or less from the peak day to bleeding;
   (c) a monophasic basal body temperature pattern;
   (d) absence of spinnbarkeit mucus; and/or
   (e) intermenstrual spotting or bleeding.

4 A woman and/or man should be advised to seek medical consultation if there is any medical history suggestive of causing impairment of the person's fertility. The couple should still attend a fertility

161

awareness class and receive guidance from the instructor. Examples of medical problems that could impare fertility are:

Female: History of pelvic infection, gonorrhea, endometriosis, extensive cryosurgery, abnormal pap smears (untreated), conization, thyroid and other endocrine dysfunctions, drug and alcohol abuse and history of stillbirths, miscarriages, repeated abortions.

Male: History of infection of the reproductive system, varicocle, genital surgery (undescended tests, hernia repairs) taking of medications, drug and alcohol abuse, exposure to toxic chemicals, heat and radiation.

Index

Note: NFP = natural family planning

Index